burgers every way

100 RECIPES USING BEEF, CHICKEN, TURKEY, LAMB, FISH, AND VEGETABLES

Emily Haft Bloom

photography by Tina Rupp

Stewart, Tabori & Chang
New York

Contents

Introduction

Americans are in the throes of a love affair. We love our big cars, our movie stars, and our burgers. Few residents of this country haven't consumed something ground up, cooked, and packed in a bun—be it beef, vegetable, lamb, grains, or things you never dreamed could be a burger. Burgers are a staple of the American diet. Once only made from ground beef and considered a fairly lowbrow food, burgers have evolved into one of the most versatile dishes to emerge from the kitchen. Both professional chefs and amateur cooks have tweaked the concept of burgers to include almost anything that can be ground up or shaped into a disk and grilled, fried, baked, or broiled. This reinvented concept in the culinary vocabulary includes ground meats like turkey, veal, pork, and game; fish, vegetables, and grains. Burgers are also the ideal food for ethnic influences; they are a blank slate just begging for flavorings and hints of international cuisines.

Once available mainly in American kitchens, drive-ins, and fast food establishments, burgers and their variations can be found on the late-night menu at the club of the moment, reinvented by the newest celebrity chef, or served in the poshest dining rooms of corporate titans and social X-rays. A burger can be grilled ground lamb in a toasted whole wheat pita pocket served with yogurt cucumber sauce and saffron-scented couscous. A burger can also be ground turkey mixed with spicy Southwestern salsa on a soft tortilla with jicama slaw. A burger can be a marinated grilled Portobello mushroom served open-faced on a slice of sprouted wheat bread with a sliver of the freshest goat cheese and heirloom tomato salad. And, for the most discriminating palate, it is even organic highest-grade ground beef stuffed with foie gras and braised short ribs! Today's burger can be the simplest form of hamburger at a fast food outpost that tastes the same from coast to coast or the most sophisticated gourmet presentation from a professional kitchen.

Over the past few years, there has been a surge of interest in developing burgers that appeal to the most discriminating diner. A perfect example of this new trend is the DB burger, created by Chef Daniel Boulud prior to his restaurant, DB Bistro Moderne's July 2001 opening in New York City. The burger is a combination of the best of American and French classic fare. The burger comes in two versions; the first and original, is made from ground sirloin and stuffed with short ribs braised in red wine, foie gras, black truffle, and root vegetables sautéed in butter, served on a homemade Parmesan and poppy seed bun. It is served with fresh horseradish, tomato confit, fresh tomato, red onions, and frisée. The DB Burger Royale, launched in January 2003, is enhanced with slices of fresh black truffle and a truffle dressing. It is only available during the black truffle season, late December through late March. The burger is served at lunch with pommes frites (French fries) and at dinner with pommes soufflés (mashed potatoes).

This burger would be challenge to prepare at home for even the most confident and accomplished cook. Perhaps a simpler less intimidating way to prepare a stuffed burger would be to marinate and grill a skirt steak until barely done and slice it thinly and mix it with a simple mélange of chopped carrot, celery, and onion sautéed in butter until soft and fragrant. Stuff ground sirloin with the blend and grill. Unless you have your own truffle dog, skip them. They are best left in the hands of the professional chef. If you must have a burger with truffles, get yourself to DB Bistro Moderne and elevate your burger consumption to a whole new level!

The increasing availability of the freshest ingredients has made making burgers that will thrill at home even easier. Home cooks are recognizing what great American chefs have known for years: the better the ingredients, the better the final product. Farm-raised beef, free-range poultry, and organic produce really do taste better. And with a little creativity and an open mind, this most beloved of American meals can become a culinary adventure for every cook.

User's Guide for *Burgers Every Way*

This book is divided into sections based on the primary burger ingredient. Each section is divided into five menus, each of which includes a burger, a beverage recipe or beer or wine recommendation, suggested breads or rolls, and side dish and condiment recipes. I sought to include side dishes that would complement each burger's flavors, ethnic influence, or style. Feel free, however, to mix and match based on your own tastes and preferences. Many of the side dishes are most suitable for warm weather and the freshest produce. If, for example, beefsteak tomatoes are called for, it's best to avoid using tomatoes altogether if the only alternative is the mushy sort found in January in your grocery store!

Each burger recipe will serve four. The side dishes also serve four but some allow for a small second helping, depending on your serving size. The condiments also are meant to serve four but some allow for either a bit left over or extra for dipping.

I am a firm believer in the theory that great tasting food doesn't have to be hard to make, so only a handful of the recipes have more than ten ingredients, none require fancy kitchen tools, and you need not have attended cooking school to make any of them.

Most burger lovers have a preferred method of preparation: grilling, pan-frying, or broiling. Personal preferences aside, some recipes are best prepared one way or another, so I've recommended a cooking method. For example, trying to cook the smoked trout burger on a grill is challenging no matter how well you handle a spatula. Most of the burgers, however, can be prepared either on a preheated outdoor gas or charcoal grill, under a preheated broiler, on an indoor electric grill, or pan-fried.

Cooking times vary based on the ingredients in the burger, the cooking method, and your heat source. Grill, gas and electric cooktops, and broiler temperatures vary during preheating and cooking, so cooking times are offered only as a guide. The thickness of your uncooked burger will also affect your cooking time. In the interest of food safety (see page 7), be careful not to serve undercooked meat, poultry, or fish.

A Word About Drinks

Each menu includes a drink suggestion, either a suitable wine or beer selection or a recipe for a drinkable accompaniment, most of which do not contain alcohol. Recipes for fruit sodas made with fresh juice and unflavored club soda or seltzer are included where wines are not; they are a festive alternative to water or colas.

Burgers, while still occupying their proud place at America's picnic tables and kitchen dinettes, have found a home in the dining room too, which makes them ideal candidates for creative wine pairing. Don't be afraid to try something unusual or what may seem like an unlikely choice. Wines can mirror a flavor or contrast it, and can greatly enhance the culinary experience. All of the suggested wines work well with the main burger ingredient, a primary seasoning, or a side dish. Better still, most suggested varieties can be found for less than $20. If you are unsure of what wine to serve with your burgers, check with your local wine shop. Just tell them what you're making and what kind of wine you have enjoyed in the past.

A Brief History of the Burger

Burger has become a household word. Most American children can request one by name by the time they are three. Americans eat three hamburgers per week per person, according to *The American Dictionary of Food and Drink*. That's 38 billion annually, or 59 percent of all sandwiches consumed, and that number doesn't include the millions of burgers made from ingredients other than ground beef.

But when did burgers enter into our daily vocabulary? Where did the idea come from? In nineteenth-century England, the nutrition expert J. H. Salisbury claimed minced beef was so nutritious that it should be consumed at least three times a day. He took the idea of mincing beef from German immigrants. The dish was especially popular in Hamburg, and consequently came to be known as "Hamburg steak." (The word burger is German in origin and means a resident of a town or "burgh.") One of the earliest descriptions of Hamburg steak in America was in 1884, in the *Boston Evening Journal*, but the term "hamburger" appeared on a menu (believed to be printed in 1834) at Delmonico's in New York City.

By 1912, ground meat patties were being served in buns, and according to *The American Dictionary of American Slang*, the suffix "burger" came to mean "any hot sandwich served on a bun, often toasted, with many condiments." But many food historians believe the man responsible for giving what we now call a burger its beloved look was J. Walter Anderson, a Wichita, Kansas resident who went on to co-found White Castle Hamburgers in 1921, the oldest continuously operating burger chain. White Castle introduced the concept of a square burger quite small in size and the idea of eating several small ones instead of one large one. The chain was noted for its consistent appearance in all its retail shops, and more importantly, the consistent tastes of its fare. While America was getting familiar with its new culinary darling, the Second World War ended, and automobiles brought even more Americans out of the house and into restaurants. Restaurant entrepreneurs combined these two American passions, burgers and cars, into an icon of mid-century America: the drive-in. Car hops, named so because they hopped onto the car's running boards, were the waitstaff bearing trays of burgers, fries, and cola.

When a restaurant equipment salesman named Kroc joined forces with two brothers named McDonald, the fast food burger was truly born. Other chains followed, both regional and national, and eventually, the fast food burger became one of the best known American exports.

As the love affair grew more intense, and the American diet more diverse, burgers morphed into sandwiches made from almost anything that could roughly approximate the size of a bun. When awareness about fat content became an obsession in the seventies, diners began to offer turkey burgers and ground turkey became available at the grocery store. Ground chicken soon followed. Ground pork, usually purchased with the intention of making sausages, or Italian-style "gravy," seemed a likely addition to the burger cook's repertoire. Enterprising chefs, realizing that Americans love their burgers with a passion, began to introduce the idea of fish, chicken, and even vegetables on a bun. Salmon burgers appealed to those who loved the idea of a burger but preferred not to eat meat. No one is quite sure when Portobello mushrooms first appeared inside a bun, but now the Portobello mushroom burger, grilled over a hot fire, is popular barbecue fare even among those who don't eschew meat in their diets.

While many Americans have tried meatless burgers, few have found them to bear any resemblance to beef burgers. The texture of a ground beef burger is hard to duplicate, but it is possible to prepare a vegetarian burger that tastes great, has a satisfying texture, and can erase the longing most vegetarians feel at one time or another for a beef burger. Chickpeas and mushrooms lend themselves well to flavors and spices and should not be overlooked by any home chef.

Food Safety

Over the past ten years, anyone who cooks at home has noticed the proliferation of warnings on food packaging, particularly on raw meat and poultry. We have all been made aware of how a little more attention to preparation and longer cooking times can greatly reduce our chances of contracting a food-borne illness. But, while we willingly forgo the raw egg in our Caesar salad, many of us are loath to part with our rare burger. There is certainly something to be said about a burger that's charred on the outside, bearing the trademark stripe of a charcoal grill, and salmon pink on the inside, barely warm and slightly mushy. It is, however, safer, wiser,

and just plain smarter to leave it on the grill for a just a minute or two more to assure yourself that this burger is safe to eat. Properly seasoned and moistened with a few selected ingredients assures that your burger won't be dry and tasteless, nor will it make you sick. Burgers made from ground poultry too need to reach a certain temperature before consumption. They can be a bit trickier as their reduced fat level makes them more likely to look and feel done sooner than they are. Use common sense; if it's still clucking, or juices run pink, leave it on for another minute!

Food Safety Precautions for Meat, Poultry, and Seafood

Below are basic food safety guidelines reprinted from the USFDA Center for Food Safety and Applied Nutrition website at www.foodsafety.gov.

o Always wash hands, cutting boards, dishes, and utensils with hot, soapy water before and after they come in contact with raw meat, poultry, or seafood.

o Separate raw meat, poultry, and seafood from other foods in your grocery shopping cart, refrigerator, and while preparing and handling foods at home.

o If possible, use one cutting board for raw meat products and another one for fresh fruits and vegetables.

o Place cooked food on a clean plate. If you put cooked food on an unwashed plate that previously held raw meat, poultry, or seafood, bacteria from the raw food could contaminate the cooked food.

o Don't use sauce that was used to marinate raw meat, poultry, or seafood on cooked foods, unless it is boiled before applying.

o Cook raw meat, poultry, and seafood to safe internal temperatures. Use a clean food thermometer to check, and wash it with hot, soapy water between uses.

o Meat can have harmful bacteria on the surface from the slaughter process, equipment from the processing plant, or germs on hands, utensils, or kitchen surfaces. When meat is "ground up" at the supermarket and handled at home, these surface bacteria can end up inside the meat.

Guidelines for Internal Temperatures

Proper cooking will kill harmful bacteria on the surface of a solid cut of meat, such as steak, because the surface gets direct heat. However, harmful bacteria on the inside of the meat are less likely to be killed by cooking if proper internal temperatures are not achieved. That's why it's important to be especially careful that the internal temperature of ground meat reaches a high enough degree to kill bacteria. To destroy harmful bacteria that may be present in ground meat, all consumers should cook ground meat to at least 160°F (71°C). Use an accurate, instant-read food thermometer to check. Make sure the food thermometer goes straight into the meat, but does not come out the other side and touch the pan.

The Centers for Disease Control and Prevention link eating undercooked, pink ground beef with a higher risk of illness. If a thermometer is not available, do not eat ground beef that is still pink inside. All foods below should reach the listed internal temperature before they are consumed.

160°F	Ground beef, veal, lamb, pork, and venison
165°F	Ground chicken and turkey

A tip for all the recipes in this book: Don't make the burgers too thick. Though you may be tempted to make them three inches high, it is nearly impossible to cook such thick burgers thoroughly without drying out the edges and the areas that come into direct contact with the cooking surface or heat. So, for safety and great taste, after you form the burgers, smush them down a little, but not too much. A good standard is that no burger (except veggie burgers with no meat ingredients) should be thicker than an inch and a half at its thickest point.

Burger Basics

Almost anyone can make a great burger, even those who claim they can't boil water! Armed with this book and a modicum of gray matter, anyone can prepare a tasty, creative and memorable meal. While recipes for themed burgers abound, and a creative chef can find accompaniments for each with ease thanks to the Internet, it is really quite easy to come up with your own versions of classics and new twists. Unlike recipes for traditional dishes and many ethnic specialties, burger recipes can be tweaked to accommodate even the most unusual culinary preferences. The simple addition of a different cheese melted on top, an ethnic spice mixed in during preparation, or an artisan baked bread as a roll can change the flavor and presentation entirely. Below is a list of standard seasonings that can be added to the basic burger. Amounts added are entirely up to the cook. It's best to add these flavors a few hours before cooking.

Just be sure to cover well and refrigerate after preparing, until you are ready to cook.

A little piece of advice I give friends who are looking for a little culinary inspiration: Open the cabinet where you keep your spices and seasonings. Take the ones in the back and move them to the front and take the ones you use all the time (like garlic powder, paprika, lemon pepper, and dill) and move them to the back. You will be amazed how much more varied your repertoire will become!

Try these different spices and flavorings:

minced garlic

minced onion

minced bell pepper

minced jalapeño pepper

minced mild green chiles

minced olives

grated Parmesan cheese

mixed fresh chopped herbs like basil, parsley, cilantro, or dill

dried herbs like cumin, paprika, oregano, sage, rosemary

seasoned breadcrumbs

soy sauce

Worcestershire sauce

barbecue sauce

any cheese, grated or chopped

prepared sun-dried tomatoes

roasted peppers (prepared or fresh)

sesame tahini

Try these different kinds of breads:

soft flatbreads or other Middle Eastern breads and rolls

pita pockets

soft tortillas

seven-grain rolls or buns

kaiser rolls

focaccia

cheese rolls

potato rolls

vegetable rolls

onion rolls

sprouted wheat rolls

cornbread

French bread

Italian bread

And instead of the usual tomato ketchup and sweet relish, keep a few of these condiments on hand for a nice change from the ordinary. Some of these are more appropriate for burgers made from poultry.

chutneys (cranberry and mango are easy to find)

roasted peppers (prepared or fresh)

salsas (tomato, mango, pineapple)

bean spreads

pestos (basil, arugula, olive, coriander)

tahini, hummus, baba ghanouj, and other Middle Eastern spreads

aïoli (garlic mayonnaise)

tapenades

barbecue sauces

spicy ketchups

soft cheese spreads

unusual hard cheeses, such as Edam

honey mustards and other variations on traditional brown mustard

Equipment

While there are no hard and fast rules about what you need to make a great burger, there are a few items that will make preparation and cooking easier and food tastier. You do not need a $4,000 outdoor grill with eight burners, a rotisserie, and digital temperature settings, nor do you need an imported French cast-iron monstrosity that's bigger than most Manhattan studios. What you do need, however, is a really good spatula. I like an offset long wooden handle with a metal blade (not recommended for nonstick pans).

A gas cooktop or grill If you have an electric stove, consider a gas grill providing you have an outside space. Charcoal grills are wonderful, but they take a bit of preparation time to heat up, so if you are looking for time-saving techniques, gas is the way to go. Most burgers can be broiled, so a clean working broiler is helpful too.

A cast-iron or heavy steel pan, well seasoned and spacious enough to prepare a burger for each member of your family at the same time. A seasoned pan means that it has been used for a while and has a shiny appearance on the inside. A well-fitting lid is a plus too, as covering the burger in the last minute of cooking tends to make the burger moister and melts cheeses evenly. Nonstick pans are great when cleaning up, and for burgers that have a hard time sticking together.

A good-quality broiling pan I prefer a heavy pan that can be lined with foil to ease with clean-up. It's best to save broiling for fattier meats, as leaner ones can dry out when broiled.

A large glass bowl or, ideally, a nesting set They clean up easily and you can see whether all your ingredients are mixed in!

Vegetable oil cooking spray Some burgers, primarily those made with fish and grains, just seem to collapse when turned. A quick shot of vegetable oil spray will help them slip off their cooking surface better and help hold it together, so to speak. Have a can nearby to avoid burger collapses.

Culinary curiosity Don't be afraid to try the stuff you never thought you'd eat, or mix in a condiment you never used before. Culinary adventures are safe, legal, and fun!

For many home cooks, buying ground beef is a simple proposition. They head to the grocery store and grab a package of ground beef. However, one secret to a good burger is a little bit of fat. Although it may be tempting to use ground sirloin, for the juiciest burger, you should always choose ground chuck. It is much harder to overcook and dry out, and the higher fat content helps make it more flavorful. Ground chuck should be no more than 85 percent lean: Most of the fat will drain off during cooking.

Your other primary concern should be freshness. The fresher the beef, the better it will taste. Many supermarkets have in-store butchers who will be happy to tell you when the beef was ground. They might even grind it for you while you shop. If you buy beef straight from the bin and it happens to smell "off" when you open the package, store it in a sealable bag and return it to the grocery for a replacement. Many stores now offer prepackaged burger meat ground that day; ask about it at your store. You can taste the difference.

Kosher beef is a costlier alternative, but it provides greater assurance of purity. Animals are inspected after slaughter to ensure that they were healthy, and the meat is handled according to strict guidelines. It is soaked and rinsed in salt and certain veins and some of the fat are removed.

Lately many supermarkets have started carrying all-natural or organic grass-fed beef. According to the United States Department of Agriculture, natural beef is beef that is "minimally processed and contains no artificial ingredients," like the hormones and antibiotics fed to feedlot cattle. If it's available to you, all-natural beef is preferable and worth the extra expense. However, kosher or organic beef is by no means necessary to the preparation of a superb hamburger. ○

Sink your teeth into an inch-thick **beef** burger, emblazoned with those cool grill stripes, and savor the juices dripping down your chin.

The Nobby Burger

Nob Hill Bar and Grill   937 NW 23rd Avenue   Portland, Oregon   Tel (503) 274-9616

8 slices thick-cut bacon

1 pound ground chuck

Salt and pepper to taste

1 tablespoon unsalted butter

4 kaiser-style rolls

4 slices sharp cheddar or pepper Jack
(for a spicier flavor)

3 tablespoons Secret Sauce (4 parts
mayonnaise and 1 part red relish)

2 tablespoons chopped Vidalia or other
sweet onion

8 crisp dill pickle chips

1 cup chopped iceberg lettuce,
patted dry and chilled

4 slices beefsteak tomatoes

The Nob Hill Bar and Grill is a low-key neighborhood joint deep in the heart of Portland, Oregon. Legions of fans return again and again for its basic burger and the more than ten variations guaranteed to satisfy any burger lover. These burgers are as unpretentious and unassuming as a grilled cheese sandwich—and that is a large part of their charm. The Nobby Burger's flavor depends on the correct layering of the ingredients. For best results, follow the sequence with care.

Preheat a gas or charcoal grill to medium-high heat and cook the bacon until crisp. Form the ground beef into 4 flat patties of equal size, and season with salt and pepper to taste. Grill the burgers, flipping once, until cooked through, about 4 minutes on each side. Butter the bottoms of the hamburger buns and, 1 minute before the burgers are done, toast both halves of the buns on the grill.

While the burgers are still on the grill, top each patty with a slice of cheese and a slice of bacon.

Quickly remove the burgers from the grill and assemble as follows:

1 Bottom bun

2 Secret Sauce

3 Sweet onions

4 Dill pickle chips

5 Iceberg lettuce

6 Tomato slice

7 Beef patty with cheese
   and bacon

8 Top bun

Don't mess with this one too much. Hint: The flatter the burger, the more evenly it will cook. This doesn't mean that your burgers need to be thin, just that they should not be rounded on top. Be gentle with the meat, though; too much handling will compact it and dry it out. On a hot summer day, you can substitute a potato salad for the giant french fries. In winter, serve these burgers with fresh mozzarella and red onion slices.

All-American Beef Burgers

MENU

○ **to eat**

All-American beef burgers on seeded kaiser rolls

Sliced beefsteak tomatoes and Vidalia onions

Monster fries

Homemade ketchup

Selection of pickles, relishes, and mustards

○ **to drink**

Merlot, also known as "the hamburger wine"

serves 4

Beef Burgers

1 1/2 pounds ground chuck

Sea salt and freshly ground black pepper to taste

Vegetable oil cooking spray

Mix together the ground beef, salt, and pepper in a large bowl using your hands or a wooden spoon. Form into 4 patties of equal size and chill for about 1 hour.

Before lighting the charcoal or gas grill, spray the racks with the cooking spray. Preheat the grill to medium-high heat and grill the burgers, flipping once, until cooked through, about 5 minutes on the first side and 4 minutes on the second.

Serve on seeded kaiser rolls with beefsteak tomato and Vidalia onion slices. Pair with homemade ketchup and a selection of pickles, relishes, and mustards.

13

Homemade Ketchup

2 small yellow onions, chopped

2 cloves garlic, finely chopped

Two 28-ounce cans crushed tomatoes (preferably San Marzano), drained

$1/2$ cup sugar

$1/2$ cup cider vinegar

1 teaspoon dry mustard

Sea salt and freshly ground black pepper to taste

Hot pepper sauce (optional)

Monster Fries

4 tablespoons ($1/2$ stick) unsalted butter

$1/4$ cup extra-virgin olive oil

$1/4$ teaspoon each of the following seasonings: sea salt, ground cumin, garlic powder, and freshly ground black pepper

4 large Idaho potatoes (about $1 1/2$ pounds), peeled

Preheat the oven to 450°F. Melt the butter in a small saucepan over low heat and stir in the olive oil and seasonings. Cut each potato in half lengthwise, then cut each half into 4 thick wedges. Brush the melted butter and oil mixture on the potato wedges to thoroughly coat. Arrange them on a cookie sheet in a single layer. Bake for about 30 minutes, turning once, until the fries are golden and crisp.

Combine the onions, garlic, and tomatoes in a large heavy-bottomed pot. Simmer over low heat for about 1 hour, stirring occasionally to loosen any bits stuck to the bottom of the pot. Using an immersion mixer, carefully puree the hot mixture until smooth. Add the sugar and vinegar and return to a simmer, stirring frequently, for about 30 minutes, until the ketchup thickens. Stir in the mustard and salt and pepper to taste. Add hot pepper sauce, if desired.

If your food processor hasn't seen the light of day since you got it, pesto is a great recipe to start with. You'll need plenty of fresh basil, best-quality Parmesan and olive oil, and pine nuts. For the bread, you can use anything from genuine Bronx's Arthur Avenue-style Italian bread to grocery-baked loaves. Take care not to cut the slices too thick or you won't taste anything but the bread. The perfect accompaniment: a platter of marinated artichoke hearts, roasted red peppers, and bocconcini (small balls of fresh mozzarella and crushed red pepper flakes in olive oil).

Pesto Burgers

MENU

o **to eat**

Pesto burgers on Italian bread

Chopped arugula and yellow tomato salad with toasted pine nuts

Marinated artichoke hearts, store-bought roasted red peppers, and mozzarella bocconcini

o **to drink**

Sangiovese, an earthy Italian red

serves 4

Pesto Burgers

1 pound ground chuck

$1/2$ cup plus 2 tablespoons homemade Basil Pesto (recipe follows) or best-quality store-bought pesto

$1/4$ cup dry Italian-flavored breadcrumbs

1 tablespoon dried oregano

2 tablespoons finely chopped red bell pepper

Sea salt and freshly ground black pepper to taste

8 slices Italian bread

Preheat a charcoal or gas grill to medium-high heat. Using your hands or a wooden spoon, mix together the ground beef, $1/2$ cup of pesto, the breadcrumbs, oregano, and red pepper in a large bowl, until the ingredients are evenly distributed. Form 4 patties of equal size and season lightly with salt and pepper. Grill for 5 minutes on the first side, then flip and press down lightly, and cook for 5 minutes more, until cooked through.

Thinly spread 2 tablespoons of the pesto on the bread slices and, 1 minute before the burgers are done, toast the bread on the grill. Drizzle the burgers with additional pesto and serve them on the toasted pesto bread.

15

Basil Pesto

2 cups fresh basil leaves (stems discarded), washed and thoroughly dried

3/4 cup pine nuts

3/4 cup freshly grated Parmesan

2 cloves garlic

Sea salt and freshly ground black pepper to taste

1 1/4 cups extra-virgin olive oil

Combine the basil, pine nuts, cheese, garlic, and salt and pepper in a food processor fitted with a steel blade. Slowly add the olive oil through the feed tube and pulse the processor on and off for 30 seconds. Stop the processor, remove the lid, and scrape down the sides with a rubber spatula. Replace the lid and pulse for 10 seconds more, until the pesto is well blended. It may be refrigerated in a sealed container for 1 week.

Chopped Arugula and Yellow Tomato Salad with Toasted Pine Nuts

2 tablespoons pine nuts

2 bunches arugula, roots discarded, washed and dried

2 yellow tomatoes, cored and diced

3 tablespoons balsamic vinegar

1/4 cup extra-virgin olive oil

Sea salt and freshly ground black pepper to taste

Preheat the oven to 350°F. Spread the pine nuts on a cookie sheet and toast for 5 minutes. Transfer to a plate to cool. Rip the arugula into 1-inch pieces and toss with the diced tomatoes in a serving bowl.

In a separate bowl, whisk together the vinegar, olive oil, and salt and pepper. Just before serving, pour the dressing over the arugula and tomatoes. Top with the toasted pine nuts.

These rib-sticking meat loaf burgers are all-American food at its best. And like all the best meat loaves, they taste even better as a sandwich the next day. I recommend using a combination of ground meats—roughly a third each of beef, veal, and pork—but feel free to experiment according to your preferences. To reduce fat, you may substitute ground turkey for any of the above meats.

Everything Burgers

MENU

o **to eat**

Everything burgers on deli-style onion rolls

Garlic mashed potatoes

Green beans with roasted tomatoes

o **to drink**

Shiraz, an Australian red

serves 4

Everything Burgers

2 slices Italian or French bread

1 tablespoon unsalted butter

1 yellow onion, chopped

1 clove garlic, minced

$1/3$ pound ground chuck

$1/3$ pound ground veal

$1/3$ pound ground pork

1 tablespoon unseasoned tomato paste

$1/4$ cup freshly grated Parmigiano-Reggiano

Sea salt and freshly ground black pepper to taste

1 large egg, lightly beaten

4 deli-style onion rolls

17

Preheat the oven to 400°F. Toast the bread on both sides until completely dry and lightly browned, checking often to avoid burning. Cool and process in a blender or food processor to form fine breadcrumbs. Meanwhile, heat the butter in a small saucepan over medium heat. Add the onion and garlic and sauté, stirring often, until fragrant and lightly browned. Using your hands or a wooden spoon, mix together the breadcrumbs, ground meats, sautéed onion and garlic, tomato paste, and grated cheese in a large bowl, until the ingredients are evenly distributed. Season with salt and pepper. Add the beaten egg and mix well. Cover with plastic wrap and refrigerate for 1 hour.

Preheat a broiler or a charcoal or gas grill to medium-high heat. Form 4 patties of equal size and grill them, flipping once, until cooked through, about 5 minutes on each side. Split the deli rolls in half and, 1 minute before the burgers are done, toast them on the grill. Serve on the toasted rolls.

18

Garlic Mashed Potatoes

1/2 head garlic, unpeeled

2 pounds Idaho potatoes

4 tablespoons (1/2 stick) unsalted butter

1/2 cup half-and-half

Sea salt and freshly ground white pepper to taste

Preheat the oven to 400°F. Wrap the garlic in one layer of aluminum foil and roast until it is soft and tender, about 45 minutes. Cool briefly then squeeze the garlic pulp from each clove and set aside.

Peel the potatoes and slice each potato crosswise into 8 pieces. Place in a large pot and cover with cold water. Bring to a boil then lower the heat and simmer until the potatoes are soft, about 15 minutes. Remove with a slotted spoon and transfer to a large deep bowl. Using a potato masher or ricer, mash the potatoes until smooth. Quickly stir in the roasted garlic, butter, and half-and-half. Season with salt and pepper and mix thoroughly. Serve hot.

Green Beans with Roasted Tomatoes

5 plum tomatoes, sliced crosswise

Sea salt and freshly black ground pepper to taste

4 ounces fresh green beans, trimmed and washed

1/4 teaspoon fresh lemon juice, or more to taste

3 scallions, white part only, thinly sliced

2 tablespoons olive oil, plus more for greasing baking sheet

Preheat the oven to 450°F. Arrange the tomato slices on a lightly greased baking sheet so they form a single layer. Season with salt and pepper. Roast on the top rack of the oven for about 10 minutes, turning the tomatoes once about halfway through the cooking time.

While the tomatoes are roasting, bring a saucepan of water to a boil and add 1 teaspoon salt. Boil the green beans until tender but still crisp, 2 to 4 minutes. Quickly drain in a colander and rinse with cold water to stop the cooking process.

Combine the roasted tomatoes and green beans in a serving bowl and toss with the lemon juice, sliced scallions, and olive oil. Season with more salt and pepper to taste. Serve at room temperature or chilled.

For those who aren't faint of palate, the heat in these burgers can be turned up to high. Base your choice of sausage on the tastes of your fellow diners, and don't be afraid to experiment. I have made these burgers with five different kinds of sausage, including very hot Italian pork sausage, smoky andouille, fennel and artichoke sausage, and as a lower fat alternative, turkey sausage. Since the cooked sausages provide ample fat, a slightly leaner ground beef may be used for these burgers. For a summer meal, replace the ratatouille with corn relish seasoned with cumin.

Spicy Beef, Sausage, and Pepper Burgers

MENU

o **to eat**

Spicy beef, sausage, and pepper burgers on Roasted red pepper bread

Classic ratatouille

o **to drink**

Ice cold beer, preferably Corona or another light-colored import

serves 4

Spicy Beef, Sausage, and Pepper Burgers

1/2 pound spicy pork sausages

1 pound ground chuck

1 yellow onion, chopped

1 clove garlic, minced

1 tablespoon minced fresh Italian parsley

Sea salt and freshly ground black pepper to taste

1/4 cup freshly grated Parmigiano-Reggiano

1 roasted red bell pepper (see Note on page 20), cut into 4 slices

Preheat a broiler or charcoal or gas grill to medium-high heat. Split the sausage casings with a knife and crumble the ground meat in a large bowl. Using your hands or a wooden spoon, combine the ground pork, ground beef, onion, garlic, and parsley until the ingredients are evenly distributed. Season with salt and pepper.

Form the meat mixture into 4 patties of equal size. Grill until cooked through, flipping once, about 5 minutes on each side. Top the burgers with the cheese and roasted pepper slices. Serve them on warm Roasted Red Pepper Bread.

19

Roasted Red Pepper Bread

4 tablespoons (1/2 stick) unsalted butter, softened

1 roasted red bell pepper (see Note)

1 clove garlic, peeled

Sea salt and freshly ground black pepper to taste

8 slices Italian or French bread

In a food processor fitted with a steel blade, combine the butter, roasted pepper, garlic, and salt and pepper. Pulse until the mixture is smooth. Spread the flavored butter on the bread and, 1 minute before the burgers are done, warm the bread on the grill.

• Note: To roast bell peppers, preheat a broiler and place the rack in the highest position. Cut the pepper in half and remove the seeds, ribs, and stem. Lightly brush the pepper with olive oil, inside and out, and arrange it on a lightly greased baking sheet. Broil until the skins are charred, about 1 minute on each side. Let cool, then gently remove the charred skin from the pepper. The roasted pepper may be refrigerated in a sealed container for about 1 week.

Classic Ratatouille

3 tablespoons olive oil

1 yellow onion, chopped

2 cloves garlic, minced

2 small green peppers, stems and seeds removed, chopped into 1-inch cubes

2 small red peppers, stems and seeds removed, chopped into 1-inch cubes

2 medium eggplants, chopped into 1-inch cubes

4 zucchini, chopped into 1-inch cubes

4 ripe tomatoes, cored and chopped into 1-inch cubes (reserve juices)

2 tablespoons chopped fresh parsley, plus more for garnish

Sea salt and freshly ground black pepper to taste

Heat 2 tablespoons of the olive oil in a large heavy-bottomed pan. Add the onion, garlic, and green and red peppers and sauté over medium heat, stirring frequently, until the onions are translucent and the peppers are soft, about 10 minutes. Transfer to a bowl and set aside.

Heat the remaining tablespoon of the olive oil in the same pan. Add the eggplant and sauté over medium heat for about 10 minutes. Add the zucchini and sauté for another 5 minutes, until both are soft and lightly browned. Stir in the tomatoes and reserved juice and cook for about 5 more minutes, until the tomatoes are soft and the mixture has thickened. Lower heat to simmer and stir in the reserved onion-pepper mixture and the chopped parsley, and season with salt and pepper. Simmer about 15 minutes more.

Garnish the ratatouille with additional chopped parsley, if desired. Serve hot, cold, or at room temperature, as a side dish or as an appetizer topping rounds of bread.

Grab your sombrero and sunblock and pass the guacamole! This spicy burger brings the flavors of Mexico to a truly American food. Flour tortillas can be found in the prepared food aisle of most grocery stores or in Latin American markets. If your store stocks flavored flatbread for roll-up sandwiches (often found in the deli section), you can substitute any flavor that appeals to you. We sampled four-cheese flatbread with these burgers and it was fabulous! Extra salsa can be served on the side with tortilla chips.

Tex-Mex Burgers

MENU

○ **to eat**

Tex-Mex burgers on soft corn tortillas

Spicy tomato salsa

South of the border red beans and rice

Tortilla chips

○ **to drink**

Red wine sangría *(serves 8)*

serves 4

Tex-Mex Burgers

1 pound ground chuck

1 jalapeño chile pepper, seeded and minced (wear gloves when preparing)

1 cup Spicy Tomato Salsa (recipe follows)

Sea salt and freshly ground pepper to taste

4 soft corn tortillas

1 ripe avocado, pitted and sliced

$1/2$ cup shredded sharp cheddar cheese

Preheat a broiler or charcoal or gas grill to medium-high heat. Using a wooden spoon (or your hands, if you are wearing gloves), mix together the ground beef, jalapeño, $1/4$ cup of the salsa, and salt and pepper in a large bowl, until the ingredients are evenly distributed. Form into 4 patties, a little flatter and greater in diameter than a usual burger shape. Broil or grill them, flipping once, until cooked through, about 4 minutes on each side.

Place tortillas in microwave, two at a time, and cook on high for about 20 seconds. Arrange each burger on a warm tortilla and top with the avocado slices, shredded cheese, and additional salsa. Alternatively, wrap each burger and the toppings in a tortilla like a burrito. Serve with the red beans and rice and additional salsa on the side.

21

Spicy Tomato Salsa

12 plum tomatoes, seeded and diced

$1/2$ cup chopped fresh cilantro

$1/2$ cup chopped Vidalia or other sweet onion

1 tablespoon jalapeño chile pepper, seeded and minced (wear gloves when preparing)

$1/4$ cup fresh lime juice

Sea salt and freshly ground black pepper to taste

Mix all the ingredients in a small glass bowl. The salsa may be used immediately for the burgers, but chill it for at least an hour if serving it as a dip.

South of the Border Red Beans and Rice

2 tablespoons olive oil

1 medium onion, finely diced

1 large clove garlic, minced

$1/2$ green bell pepper, finely diced

$1/2$ tablespoon chili powder

1 tablespoon store-bought hot sauce

One 16-ounce can red kidney beans, drained and rinsed

2 cups hot cooked long-grain white rice

Salt and pepper to taste

Heat the olive oil in a large skillet over medium heat. Add the onions, garlic, and green pepper, and cook, stirring frequently, until the pepper is soft, about 10 minutes. Add the chili powder, hot sauce, and kidney beans, and simmer about 10 minutes, or until hot. Mix in the cooked rice, season with salt and pepper, and serve.

Red Wine Sangría

4 cups red wine

2 cups lemon- or lime-flavored seltzer water

$1/2$ cup fresh orange juice

$1/4$ cup sugar

1 tablespoon orange liqueur

1 tablespoon fresh lemon juice

1 tablespoon fresh lime juice

1 lemon, thinly sliced

1 lime, thinly sliced

Combine all the ingredients in a large pitcher, stirring until all the sugar is dissolved. Chill for at least 1 hour. Pour into tall glasses filled with ice.

23

I remember when turkey burgers were first discovered by the fat-phobic in the seventies. These dry, tasteless, fat-free patties were served on a bed of chopped iceberg lettuce without a bun. Visually, they were an unappetizing beige color that seemed like culinary purgatory. I ate my share and always found them wanting . . . for something. The secret to moist and flavorful turkey and chicken burgers is adding enough moisture to replace the fat they lack. When we fry or broil them, fat drains out and leaves us with dry burgers. One way to remedy this is to use ground poultry that includes some dark meat, which has more flavor than the white breast meat alone. Packages labeled ground turkey are a mix of light and dark meat, while breast meat alone is labeled as all white meat. Eggs and breadcrumbs, traditionally used to moisten and bind, are also helpful, but a little imagination can add a whole lot more flavor. Adding colorful ingredients like chopped bell peppers, tomatoes, or the green parts of scallions, or fresh herbs like cilantro, dill, and rosemary, can make turkey and chicken burgers a bit more appealing to the eye as well as the palate. Before adding vegetables, sauté them for a few minutes in a tablespoon of olive oil, if time allows. Turkey burgers need an extra flavor boost, so use a heavier hand with fresh herbs. I added a duck burger at the end of this chapter, because though it isn't ground, I couldn't resist sharing my favorite sandwich.○

The secret to moist and flavorful **poultry** burgers is adding the right ingredients to keep them from tasting like a cardboard box.

Herbed Chicken Burgers *p27*

Rosemary Turkey Burgers

Mustard Seed Café   1948 Hillhurst Avenue   Los Feliz, California   Tel (323) 660-0670

1 pound ground turkey (preferably a mixture of light and dark meat)

2 tablespoons plus 1 teaspoon finely chopped fresh rosemary

2 tablespoons mayonnaise or plain low-fat yogurt

1 tablespoon Worcestershire sauce

2 tablespoons salted butter

1 red onion, thinly sliced

Sea salt and freshly ground black pepper to taste

1 cup Herbed Aïoli (recipe follows)

4 leaves romaine lettuce, chilled

4 tablespoons chopped ripe tomatoes

8 slices rosemary sourdough bread

Although the Mustard Seed Café in the Los Feliz neighborhood of Los Angeles is little known outside the area, its Rosemary Turkey Burgers have earned many compliments. Although there is no secret ingredient, the rosemary sourdough bread it is served on makes all the difference. Since keeping ground turkey moist is a challenge, this recipe calls for the addition of 2 tablespoons mayonnaise. Those watching their fat intake can substitute yogurt flavored with a pinch of extra rosemary. Because you may not be able to locate rosemary sourdough bread, consider using sliced sourdough bread spread with a mixture of 2 tablespoons butter or margarine and 1/2 tablespoon chopped fresh rosemary. Place it under a broiler or on the grill for 1 minute to toast.

Preheat a broiler or charcoal or gas grill to medium-high heat. Using your hands or a wooden spoon, mix together the ground turkey, 2 tablespoons rosemary, mayonnaise, and Worcestershire sauce in a large bowl, until the ingredients are evenly distributed. Form into 4 flat burgers of equal size and set aside.

Melt the butter in a small saucepan, add the onion slices, and simmer until soft, about 10 minutes. Season with salt and pepper. Remove the onions from the pan and set aside. Stir the remaining 1 teaspoon rosemary into the melted butter and remove from heat.

Broil or grill the burgers, flipping once, until cooked through, 4 to 5 minutes on each side. Spread the rosemary butter on each slice of bread and, 1 minute before the burgers are done, toast the bread under the broiler or on the grill. Serve the burgers between the toasted rosemary bread, topped with the Herbed Aïoli, lettuce, sautéed red onion, and chopped tomato. Cut the burgers in half before serving.

Herbed Aïoli

3/4 cup mayonnaise
1 clove garlic, minced
2 teaspoons chopped fresh rosemary
2 teaspoons Dijon mustard
1 tablespoon fresh lemon juice
1 tablespoon balsamic vinegar
Sea salt and freshly ground black pepper to taste

Whisk all the ingredients in a small bowl until well blended.

26

These simple, tasty burgers are a favorite in my kitchen. If you have some ground chicken and a selection of fresh herbs, you can whip up a meal fit for your mother-in-law in 10 minutes. Use whatever fresh herbs catch your eye; they'll keep for a week if you wrap them in a damp paper towel. You can substitute dry herbs in a pinch, but use only half as much as the recipe calls for since their flavor is stronger. In the summer, I prefer a cool salad with this burger. In the winter, an herbed chicken burger (sans bun) served on a bed of seasoned pasta is a delicious dinner.

Herbed Chicken Burgers

MENU

o **to eat**

Herbed chicken burgers on Italian semolina bread

Mustard-dill mayonnaise

Penne with artichoke hearts and sun-dried tomatoes

o **to drink**

Fresh-squeezed lemonade

serves 4

Chicken Burgers

1 pound ground chicken (preferably a mixture of light and dark meat)

$1/4$ cup chopped fresh herbs (equal parts parsley, chives, dill, and tarragon is nice)

1 large egg, lightly beaten

$1/2$ cup chopped Vidalia or other sweet onion

$1/2$ cup dry Italian-flavored breadcrumbs

1 clove garlic, minced

Sea salt and freshly ground black pepper to taste

Preheat the broiler or a charcoal or gas grill to medium-high heat. Using your hands or a wooden spoon, mix together all the ingredients in a large bowl until evenly distributed. Form 4 patties of equal size. Broil or grill them, flipping once, until cooked through, about 4 minutes on each side. Serve the burgers on semolina bread, topped with the Mustard-Dill Mayonnaise. Serve additional mayonnaise and the Penne with Artichoke Hearts and Sun-dried Tomatoes on the side.

27

Mustard-Dill Mayonnaise

3/4 cup mayonnaise

2 tablespoons chopped fresh dill

1 tablespoon Dijon mustard

Sea salt and freshly ground black pepper to taste

Whisk together the mayonnaise, dill, and mustard in a small glass bowl. Season with salt and pepper.

Penne with Artichoke Hearts and Sun-dried Tomatoes

8 ounces pasta, preferably penne or rotini

1/4 cup good-quality olive oil

1 1/2 cups coarsely chopped Italian-style artichoke hearts

3/4 cup sun-dried tomatoes, chopped coarsely

1 teaspoon lemon pepper

Sea salt and freshly ground black pepper to taste

1/4 cup freshly grated good quality Parmesan

Cook the pasta according to package directions until al dente. While the pasta is cooking, heat the olive oil in a saucepan over low heat, and add the artichoke hearts and sun-dried tomatoes, stirring frequently. When the pasta is done, drain in a colander and return to the cooking pot. Add the warm artichoke and sun-dried tomato mixture. Season with the lemon pepper and salt and black pepper, tossing to combine. Sprinkle with the cheese and serve warm.

Fresh-Squeezed Lemonade

8 cups cold water

1/4 cup freshly squeezed lemon juice

4 thin lemon slices

1/2 cup sugar

1 teaspoon grated lemon zest

Lemon wedges, for garnish

In a large glass pitcher, combine the cold water, lemon juice, lemon slices, sugar, and lemon zest. Mix until the sugar dissolves. Serve in tall glasses over ice. Garnish with lemon wedges.

Indian cuisine and ground poultry seem made for each other: The naturally bland flavor of turkey begs for the delicious aroma of curry. If you are not a fan of spicy food, don't turn the page yet. Curry can be searingly hot or mild, depending on the variety you choose. In fact, the curry powder sold in the spice aisle at your local grocery store is probably not going to knock your socks off. If you can't handle hot food, try using one-half the curry powder to start. Naan is an Indian flatbread that can be found at many deli counters. Since naan usually comes in one big oval piece, fold it around the burger for easier eating.

Curry in a Hurry Burgers

MENU

o **to eat**

Curry in a hurry burgers on warmed naan

Basmati rice with cashews and currants

Pineapple chutney

Sliced tomatoes, chopped lettuce, and chopped onion, for garnish

o **to drink**

Pineapple cooler

serves 4

Curry Burgers

1 pound ground turkey (preferably a mixture of light and dark meat)

1/2 cup sour cream

1/4 cup chopped red onion

2 tablespoons curry powder (mild or hot)

2 teaspoons chopped fresh mint

Sea salt and freshly ground black pepper to taste

Olive oil, for greasing pan

1/4 cup Pineapple Chutney (recipe follows)

29

Using your hands or a wooden spoon, mix together the ground turkey, 1/4 cup of the sour cream, onion, 1 tablespoon of the curry, and 1 teaspoon of the mint in a large bowl, until the ingredients are evenly distributed. Season with salt and pepper. Form into 4 patties of equal size. Lightly grease a large skillet with olive oil. Pan-fry the burgers over medium heat, flipping once, until cooked through, about 4 minutes on each side. While the burgers are cooking, warm the naan in a pre-heated 350°F oven, about 5 minutes. Whisk together the remaining 1/4 cup sour cream, 1 tablespoon curry, and 1 teaspoon mint. Serve the burgers on the warm naan topped with the sour cream-curry spread and the Pineapple Chutney. Garnish with tomatoes, lettuce, and chopped onion. Serve additional chutney and the Basmati Rice with Cashews and Currants on the side.

Basmati Rice with Cashews and Currants

5 tablespoons lemon juice

3 tablespoons soy sauce

2 1/2 teaspoons ground cumin

5 tablespoons extra-virgin olive oil

4 tablespoons water

1 tablespoon dried currants
(or black raisins)

1 1/2 cups basmati or texmati rice,
cooked according to package directions

3/4 cup chopped cashews

Sea salt and freshly ground black pepper
to taste

30

Whisk together the lemon juice, soy sauce, and cumin, then add the olive oil and whisk until emulsified. Set aside. Heat the water in a small saucepan over low heat, add the currants, and simmer until they are plump, about 5 minutes. Pour the currants and soaking water into a large serving bowl, add the cooked rice, cashews, and dressing, and toss to combine. Season with salt and pepper and serve warm.

Pineapple Chutney

2 cups finely chopped fresh or canned pineapple (if using canned, choose unsweetened pineapple and drain)

1/2 cup finely chopped red onion

1/2 cup peeled and finely chopped Granny Smith apple

2 tablespoons sugar

2 tablespoons cider vinegar

Sea salt to taste

Mix together all the ingredients in a glass bowl. Cover and chill for 1 hour before serving. The chutney may be refrigerated in a sealed container for up to 3 days.

Pineapple Cooler

2 cups fresh pineapple juice
(or unsweetened store-bought juice)

4 cups unflavored seltzer

2 cups ice cubes

Fresh pineapple slices, for garnish

Combine the pineapple juice, seltzer, and ice cubes in a blender. Blend until smooth. Pour into tall glasses and garnish with the pineapple slices.

If you love Greek food (especially olives), these burgers will be a favorite. However, be sure to drain the feta cheese thoroughly or your burgers will drown and crumble somewhere between the fridge and the frying pan. For rolls, you can use olive bread or Italian bread spread with tapenade, an olive-based condiment that hails from the south of France. A recipe is provided below or you can purchase tapenade from a gourmet food store. Leftover tapenade spread on flatbread or crackers makes a nice appetizer.

Zorba Burgers

MENU

o **to eat**

Zorba burgers on Italian or olive bread

Olive tapenade

Sliced radishes and cucumbers, for the tapenade

Cucumber and onion salad

Mixed black and green olives

o **to drink**

Minted iced tea

serves 4

Zorba Burgers

1/2 cup sour cream

10 Greek olives, pitted and finely chopped

1/2 cup feta cheese, crumbled and drained into a bowl lined with a paper towel to remove all excess water

1 pound ground turkey meat (preferably a mixture of light and dark meat)

1 tablespoon chopped fresh parsley

1 clove garlic, minced

Sea salt and freshly ground black pepper to taste

8 slices Italian bread or olive bread

Olive oil, for greasing pan

Mix the sour cream with half the olives and half the feta; set aside. Using your hands or a wooden spoon, mix together the ground turkey, remaining 5 olives and 1/4 cup feta, parsley, and garlic in a large bowl, until the ingredients are evenly distributed. Season with salt and pepper. Form into 4 patties of equal size.

Lightly grease a large skillet with olive oil. Pan-fry the burger, flipping once, until cooked through, about 4 minutes on each side. Serve the burgers on Italian bread spread with a teaspoon of Olive Tapenade or olive bread. Top with the reserved olive and feta cheese spread. Serve the Cucumber and Onion Salad, along with mixed olives, on the side.

31

Olive Tapenade

1 1/2 cups small brine-cured black olives, rinsed and pitted

1/4 cup extra-virgin olive oil

1/4 cup finely chopped fresh parsley leaves

In a food processor fitted with a steel blade, pulse the olives with the olive oil until coarsely chopped. Transfer to a serving bowl and stir in the chopped parsley. Serve with crudités, such as celery stalks or cucumber and radish slices. Tapenade may be kept refrigerated in a sealed container for up to 1 week.

Cucumber and Onion Salad

3 kirby cucumbers, seeded and diced

1 small red onion, diced

4 tablespoons distilled white vinegar

2 teaspoons sugar

Sea salt and freshly ground black pepper to taste

1 tablespoon chopped fresh dill

Mix together the cucumber, onion, vinegar, and sugar in a glass bowl. Season with salt and pepper, sprinkle with the dill, and toss to combine. Serve cold or at room temperature.

Minted Iced Tea

10 cups boiling water

6 black decaffeinated tea bags

2 lemon tea bags

2 peppermint tea bags

1/2 cup sugar (optional)

Juice of 1/2 lemon

8 sprigs fresh mint plus more for garnish

Remove paper tags and staples from the tops of the tea bags and tie all the strings together. Place the tea bags and the mint sprigs in a large pitcher and pour the boiling water over them. Stir in the sugar until it dissolves, and allow the tea to steep for 1 hour, until it has cooled to room temperature.

Stir in the lemon juice and remove the tea bags and the mint, squeezing them to remove excess tea. Serve in tall glasses filled with ice. Garnish with extra sprigs of mint.

32

Ground chicken is a welcome change from the usual whole roasted bird. Kids who resist eating chicken have been known to inhale these burgers and ask for more. And before you complain about the addition of blue cheese to a chicken patty, remember what always comes with your order of chicken wings at the pub! White-meat-only ground chicken might be a little dry when cooked; a mix of light and dark meat works best. If your grocer doesn't carry ground chicken, request it, or substitute ground turkey. Vegetable chips are a favorite in my household and are a nice alternative to store-bought potato chips.

Blue Bird Burgers

MENU

o **to eat**

Blue bird burgers on poppy seed rolls

Blue onion sauce

Red cabbage slaw

Vegetable chips

o **to drink**

Gazpacho Virgin Mary

serves 4

Blue Bird Burgers

3/4 pound ground chicken (preferably a mixture of white and dark meat)

1 large egg, lightly beaten

1/2 cup crumbled blue cheese

1 cup dry unseasoned breadcrumbs

Vegetable oil cooking spray

Using your hands or a wooden spoon, mix together the ground chicken, egg, cheese, and bread-crumbs in a large bowl, until the ingredients are evenly distributed. Form into 4 patties of equal size.

Lightly spray a large skillet with cooking spray. Pan-fry the burgers over medium heat, flipping once, until cooked through, about 4 minutes on each side. Do not press down on the burgers with a spatula or they will become dry.

Serve the burgers on poppy seed rolls and top with Blue Onion Sauce. When the burgers are done, arrange each on a poppy seed roll and top with 1 tablespoon of the sauce. Serve additional sauce on the side.

33

Blue Onion Sauce

1 clove garlic, minced

2 tablespoons chopped Vidalia or other sweet onion

2 tablespoons crumbled blue cheese

1/2 cup plain low-fat yogurt

Sea salt and freshly ground black pepper to taste

Whisk together all the ingredients in a small glass bowl.

Red Cabbage Slaw

2 tablespoons mayonnaise

3 tablespoons distilled white vinegar

2 tablespoons sugar

1/2 teaspoon celery seed (optional)

1/2 red cabbage, tough outer leaves discarded, finely shredded (about 4 cups)

1/2 red onion, thinly sliced

Sea salt and freshly ground black pepper to taste

Place the mayonnaise, vinegar, sugar, and celery seed, if using, in a plastic sealable storage container. Put on the lid and shake the dressing vigorously to combine. Add the shredded cabbage and sliced onion, toss to coat thoroughly with the dressing, and season with salt and pepper. Serve chilled or at room temperature. The slaw may be kept refrigerated in a sealed container for up to 3 days.

Vegetable Chips

2 tablespoons vegetable oil

1/2 teaspoon garlic

1/4 teaspoon dried thyme

1/4 teaspoon dried oregano

1/8 teaspoon black pepper

1/2 teaspoon salt

3 cups 1/4-inch-thick slices peeled root vegetables such as parsnips, carrots, or beets (total of about 1 pound)

In a large bowl, stir together the oil, garlic, thyme, oregano, and pepper. Add vegetable slices and toss gently till well coated. Arrange in a single layer on lightly greased baking sheets. Bake in a preheated 350°F oven for 20 to 25 minutes, or until crisp and light golden brown. Serve warm.

Gazpacho Virgin Mary

4 cups vegetable juice

1 teaspoon hot pepper sauce

1 tablespoon minced cucumber

1 tablespoon minced yellow bell pepper

1 tablespoon minced grape or cherry tomatoes

Sea salt and freshly ground black pepper to taste

Celery sticks, for garnish

In a glass pitcher filled with ice, combine the vegetable juice, hot pepper sauce, cucumber, bell pepper, and tomato and stir. Pour into tall glasses. Add salt and pepper, and stir with a celery stick.

35

All right, these aren't really burgers….they are more like sandwiches. But as a big fan of roast duck, I could not resist the opportunity to include this great recipe. You can serve these orange-flavored burgers on any kind of bread, but I like using crusty French bread. The piquant flavor of cranberries has been the longtime companion of many a duck dish, so wild rice with dried cranberries is a great partner for this sandwich.

36

Orange-Flavored Shredded Duck Burgers

MENU

o to eat

Orange-flavored shredded duck burgers on French bread slices

Classic Caesar salad

Cranberry-nut rice

o to drink

An Australian Shiraz, a popular accompaniment to duck dishes

serves 4

Duck Burgers

1/4 cup sugar

1 cup water

2 tablespoons red wine vinegar

1 1/2 cups fresh orange juice

1 1/2 cups chicken stock (if using canned stock, choose a low-sodium variety)

1/4 cup (1/2 stick) unsalted butter

2 tablespoons grated orange zest

2 boneless duck breasts (about 2 pounds), halved, skin on

Combine the sugar and water in a heavy-bottomed pot over medium heat. Stir constantly to avoid scorching, increasing the heat as necessary until a syrup is formed. Remove from heat and stir in the vinegar and orange juice. Return to a boil, then lower the heat to a simmer until the mixture thickens, about 10 minutes. Add the stock and return to a boil again, then simmer gently for about 10 minutes more. Stir in the butter and grated orange peel; set aside.

While the sauce is simmering, gently pierce the duck breasts a few times with the tip of a sharp knife. Heat a large skillet over medium-high and sauté the breasts, skin side down, until crisp, about 6 minutes. Turn the breasts and sauté until cooked through, about 5 minutes more. Remove from heat and let the breasts cool slightly.

When the duck meat is cool enough to handle, shred it with a serrated knife or your fingers. Place it in a large glass bowl and add 1 cup of the orange sauce, tossing to combine. Let the mixture sit for about 15 minutes so that the flavors meld, then arrange the shredded duck on slices of French bread. Top with additional sauce, cover with another slice of bread and serve with the Classic Caesar Salad and Cranberry-Nut Rice on the side.

Classic Caesar Salad

1 clove garlic

2 tablespoons fresh lemon juice

2 tablespoons mayonnaise

Sea salt and freshly ground black pepper to taste

6 anchovy fillets, plus 4 for garnish (optional)

4 tablespoons extra-virgin olive oil

2 romaine hearts, washed and torn into small pieces

1/2 cup freshly grated Parmigiano-Reggiano

In a food processor fitted with a steel blade, combine the garlic, lemon juice, mayonnaise, salt and pepper, and 6 anchovies, if using. Pulse until smooth, then pour the olive oil through the feed tube, a little bit at a time, pulsing until the dressing is emulsified. Put the lettuce in a large salad bowl and toss with the dressing and grated cheese. Sprinkle with additional freshly ground black pepper, if desired.

Cranberry-Nut Rice

1 tablespoon vegetable oil

1 small yellow onion, minced

1 1/2 cups wild rice

1 cup water

1 cup chicken stock

3/4 cup dried cranberries

1/2 cup chopped pecans, walnuts, or hazelnuts

1 tablespoon red wine vinegar

1 teaspoon lemon pepper

Sea salt and freshly ground black pepper to taste

3 tablespoon extra-virgin olive oil

37

Heat the vegetable oil in a heavy-bottomed pot over medium heat. Sauté the onion until soft and fragrant, about 6 minutes. Add the wild rice and stir to coat. Pour in the water and bouillon and bring to a boil, then cover and reduce heat to low. Simmer until the water is absorbed and the rice is fluffy and tender, about 30 minutes. Let stand, covered, for about 10 minutes. Add the cranberries and nuts and toss to combine.

Whisk together the vinegar, lemon pepper, salt and pepper, and olive oil until emulsified. Pour the dressing over the rice. Serve at room temperature or chilled.

Many cooks think of ground veal, lamb, and pork almost exclusively as the basis for meatloaf or red sauce. But they are also versatile and delicious when used alone. Because of a higher fat content, the lamb and pork don't dry out as easily as ground poultry, which makes them an excellent alternative to ground beef. Ground veal has a more delicate flavor and color and tastes best when paired with milder flavors. Strong spices can overpower it.

Ground pork is the most readily available of the three, but if you can't find any, hot or sweet sausages may be used instead. Just cut them open with a sharp knife, slip the skins off, and use the ground meat inside. Bear in mind that many sausages are now made with flavorings like sun-dried tomatoes or broccoli rabe. If you love these flavors, then the seasoning for your burgers is built in.

Ground lamb often can be found in Middle Eastern grocers. It might also be available at a better butcher shop, but you may have to order it a few days in advance. Since ground veal is often included in meat loaf mix, you might be able to get it from your butcher before it is packaged as a blend. Just ask!

Although ground lamb is traditionally associated with Greek and Middle Eastern cuisines, it can also be paired with Italian seasonings. The stronger flavor of ground pork needs less seasoning; barbecue sauce is your best bet. Veal goes nicely with more subtle seasonings, like fresh herbs. Tiny versions of these recipes (roughly 1 pound of ground meat can make about 14 "baby" burgers) make great passed hors d'oeuvres, when paired with dipping sauces and served on small bread rounds. ○

Think of ground **veal**, **lamb**, **and pork** as a satisfying alternative to a ground beef burger. Their distinctive tastes will be a welcome addition to your burger repertoire.

Bakeman's Meatloaf Sandwich

Bakeman's Restaurant   122 Cherry Street   Seattle, Washington   Tel (206) 622-3375

1/2 pound ground chuck

1/2 pound ground veal

2 teaspoons cornstarch

1/2 large onion, grated

1 egg, lightly beaten

2 tablespoons soy sauce

1/4 cup tomato paste

4 tablespoons cracker meal
or unseasoned breadcrumbs

1 teaspoon salt

1 teaspoon garlic powder

1 teaspoon ground ginger

1 teaspoon chili powder

1 teaspoon cumin

1 teaspoon freshly ground
black pepper

Dried rosemary, thyme, and
basil to taste

Meatloaf is the most underrated food in the American kitchen. When I was growing up and carried my lunch to school every day, the best sandwich to find in my brown paper sack was my mom's meatloaf left over from the previous night's dinner. My brother's friends coveted them so much that he could literally auction these tasty sandwichs off, gathering pockets full of change and other people's lunches in exchange for parting with his.

Bakeman's, a laid-back cafeteria-style restaurant in Seattle, Washington, has a longstanding reputation for doing things right. Their breads are homemade, their turkey sandwiches are carved from turkeys roasted fresh every day, and their meatloaf sandwiches are mentioned in almost every "off the beaten track" guide to Seattle. Jason Wang has been making this meatloaf sandwich the same way for 35 years and the recipe is kept safely in his head! While some of his seasonings are traditional, a few are less obvious choices for meatloaf. He uses tomato paste and never ketchup, which contains too much sugar. Although he uses ground beef exclusively, I have added some ground veal to lighten the flavor. This recipe can be thrown together in a matter of minutes and is sure to satisfy any carnivore sitting at your dinner table.

Preheat the oven to 350°F. Using your hands or a wooden spoon, mix together all the ingredients in a large bowl until evenly distributed. Press the mixture into a loaf pan and bake until the juices run clear when poked with a knife, about 40 minutes. Let cool for about 10 minutes, then cut into 4 slices about 1 to 1 1/2 inches thick. Serve with ketchup and mustard on whole wheat buns.

Smoked cheddar's hearty flavor is an excellent addition to pork burgers. If you want, experiment with other smoked cheeses, like Gouda or mozzarella. Leave out the jalapeños if your palate isn't up to it, or replace them with some hot pepper sauce to give these burgers a little kick. These are best right off the grill, so if you have one, use it! The Potato Onion Tart offsets the strong flavors of the pork burgers. I also love the cool flavors of the coleslaw made with jicama, one of the most underrated vegetables available. If you can find it, you have to try it.

Pork Burgers with Smoked Cheddar and Hot Peppers

MENU

o **to eat**

Pork burgers with smoked cheddar and hot peppers on sourdough rolls

Spicy chili mayonnaise

Potato onion tart

Jicama slaw

o **to drink**

Mint lemonade

serves 4

Pork Burgers

1/2 pound spicy or sweet pork sausages

1/2 pound ground pork

1 tablespoon finely chopped jalapeño pepper (wear gloves when preparing)

1 tablespoon Worcestershire sauce

2 tablespoons finely chopped fresh cilantro

1/2 cup diced smoked cheddar

1/2 cup diced yellow onion

1 teaspoon cumin

1 teaspoon chopped fresh parsley

Preheat a gas or charcoal grill to medium-high heat. Split the sausage casings with a knife and crumble the ground meat into a large bowl. Add the rest of the ingredients and, using a wooden spoon or your hands (if wearing gloves), mix together until the ingredients are evenly distributed, taking care to break up the sausage meat.

Form into 4 patties of equal size. Grill the burgers, flipping once, until the juices run clear, about 4 minutes on each side. Serve on sourdough rolls topped with the Spicy Chili Mayonnaise. Serve the Potato Onion Tart and Jicama Slaw on the side.

41

Spicy Chili Mayonnaise

1 cup mayonnaise

1 teaspoon chili powder

1 teaspoon garlic powder

1 teaspoon fresh lemon juice

Whisk together all the ingredients in a small glass bowl. Cover and chill for at least 1 hour before serving.

Potato Onion Tart

4 medium Idaho potatoes (about 2 pounds), peeled

1 large Vidalia or other sweet onion, trimmed

1 tablespoon fresh lemon juice

Sea salt and freshly ground black pepper to taste

1/4 cup vegetable oil, plus more if needed

Using a food processor fitted with a grating or julienne blade, julienne the potatoes then the onion. Transfer to a large glass bowl and toss with the lemon juice. Season liberally with salt and pepper.

In a large heavy-bottomed skillet, heat the vegetable oil over medium-high heat. Add the onions, stirring often, and sauté until soft and translucent, about 4 minutes. Add the potatoes, tossing to combine with the onions and cook for 5 more minutes until potatoes become soft. Press the potato-onion mixture with an offset spatula to form a cake and distribute evenly around the pan. Reduce the heat and cook until the cake is golden brown on the bottom (use the spatula to peek), about 15 minutes. If the skillet becomes dry or the tart begins to scorch, add more oil, a teaspoon at a time. Turn the cake over and cook, adding additional oil if needed, about 10 more minutes. Remove from heat when it has browned evenly. Let cool before cutting into wedges and serving.

You can use this tart as a "bun" for the burger instead of bread. When the tart has cooled, turn the pan upside down onto a large platter and release the tart. Cut the tart into squares and place a burger on top of each square.

Jicama Slaw

1 ear corn (to make 1/2 cup kernels)

1 large jicama, peeled

1/2 cup sour cream

1/4 cup chopped scallions, both white and green parts

1/4 cup red wine vinegar

2 tablespoons chopped fresh cilantro

Sea salt and freshly ground black pepper to taste

Put 4 cups water in a medium saucepan and bring to a boil. Add the corn cob and boil for 5 minutes. Allow to cool. Remove the corn from the cob with a sharp knife. Shred the jicama with a mandoline or a food processor fitted with a grating or julienne blade.

In a large glass bowl, mix the sour cream, scallions, corn, vinegar, cilantro, and salt and pepper. Add the shredded jicama and toss well to coat with the dressing.

Mint Lemonade

3 lemons, washed and thinly sliced

1 cup mint leaves, loosely packed

1 cup sugar

6 cups water

3/4 cup fresh lemon juice

Mint leaves or lemon slices, for garnish

In a mini-chopper or food processor, pulverize the lemon slices and mint with 1/2 cup of the sugar until the lemons have released most of their juice. Pour the mixture through a fine-mesh sieve into a large glass pitcher, pressing down on the solids to release the juice. Add the water, remaining 1/2 cup sugar, and lemon juice to the pulp left in the sieve, again pressing down on the solids to release as much juice as possible. Discard the mixture in the sieve. Serve in tall glasses over ice. Garnish with mint leaves or lemon slices.

Chopped figs may seem like an odd addition to a burger, but they are delicious with ground lamb. Look for the figs packed in resealable bags as these have softer skins; Turkish figs threaded on twine are harder to chop. Chopped dates may be substituted if figs are unavailable. Middle Eastern flatbread, also called mountain or shepherd's bread, may be found in the deli section of your grocery store. When shopping for saffron, be prepared—it's pricey, but a little bit goes a long way. Its unique flavor, scent, and color make plain dishes fabulous.

Mediterranean Burger

MENU

○ **to eat**

Mediterranean burger on Middle Eastern mountain bread

Saffron sauce

Couscous salad with peas and mint

○ **to drink**

A California Syrah, an excellent and popular accompaniment to grilled lamb

serves 4

Mediterranean Burger

1 pound ground lamb

1/4 cup Calimyrna or Mission dried figs, pitted and chopped

1 clove garlic, minced

1 tablespoon paprika

1 teaspoon cumin

1 teaspoon crumbled saffron threads

1 teaspoon dried thyme

Sea salt and freshly ground black pepper to taste

Vegetable oil cooking spray

Preheat a broiler or charcoal or gas grill to medium-high heat. Using your hands or a wooden spoon, mix together the ground lamb and figs with the garlic, paprika, cumin, saffron, and thyme until the ingredients are evenly distributed. Season with salt and pepper.

Form into 4 patties of equal size and lightly spray on both sides with cooking spray. Broil or grill the burgers, flipping once, until the juices run clear, about 5 minutes on each side. Serve open-faced on Middle Eastern flatbread or on a bed of the Couscous Salad with Peas and Mint. Top with the Saffron Sauce, serving any extra sauce on the side.

43

Saffron Sauce

1 tablespoon olive oil

2 tablespoons chopped yellow onion

$1/4$ cup dry white wine

$1/4$ teaspoon crumbled saffron threads

Sea salt to taste

Heat the olive oil in a medium saucepan over medium heat. Add the onions and sauté until soft and translucent, about 8 minutes. Stir in the wine and saffron threads and simmer until the sauce is reduced by half. Season with salt and serve warm.

Couscous Salad with Peas and Mint

1 cup peas, fresh or frozen

2 tablespoons olive oil

$1/2$ cup finely chopped red bell pepper

1 clove garlic, crushed

1 cup plain couscous, prepared according to package instructions

$1/2$ cup chopped mint

1 tablespoon red wine vinegar

Sea salt and freshly ground black pepper to taste

Bring 2 cups water to a boil, add the fresh or frozen peas, and cook for 2 minutes, or until tender. Remove from heat, drain, and set aside. Heat 1 tablespoon of the olive oil in a skillet and sauté the red pepper and garlic until the pepper is soft, about 5 minutes. Place the cooked couscous in a large serving bowl and add the cooked peas, sautéed pepper and garlic mixture, and chopped mint, tossing to combine.

Whisk the vinegar with the remaining 1 tablespoon olive oil and season with salt and pepper. Pour the dressing over the couscous salad and serve warm.

Veal and Italian cuisine have enjoyed a long, passionate relationship, but ground veal is often overlooked by fans of Italian food. Serve these veal burgers with a classic Italian Chianti. Start the meal with an array of antipasti, including store-bought eggplant caponata, roasted peppers, artichoke hearts, olives, and maybe some salami, prosciutto, and crusty Italian bread. A dish of garlic-infused olive oil is great for dipping. I serve these burgers on medium-thick slices of Italian bread, brushed with garlic butter and toasted under a broiler or on a hot grill for a minute or two. Mangia!

Veal Parmesan Burgers

MENU

○ **to eat**

Antipasto platter

Veal Parmesan Burgers on crusty Italian bread

Tomato and broccoli rabe sauté

○ **to drink**

A classic Italian menu deserves a classic Italian wine, such as a fruity, lush Chianti.

serves 4

Veal Parmesan Burgers

1 pound ground veal

1/4 cup crushed tomatoes

1/4 cup freshly grated Parmigiano-Reggiano

1 clove garlic, minced

1 teaspoon dried oregano

Sea salt and freshly ground black pepper to taste

Slivers of Parmigiano-Reggiano

Preheat a charcoal or gas grill to medium-high heat. Using your hands or a wooden spoon, mix together the ground veal, tomatoes, grated cheese, garlic, oregano, and salt and pepper in a large bowl, until the ingredients are evenly distributed. Form into 4 patties of equal size.

Grill the burgers, flipping once, until the juices run clear, 4 minutes on each side. Serve on crusty Italian bread, spread with garlic butter topped with the Parmigiano-Reggiano and with the Tomato and Broccoli Rabe Sauté on the side.

45

Tomato and Broccoli Rabe Sauté

1/4 cup extra-virgin olive oil

2 cloves garlic, smashed with the flat side of a large knife

4 plum tomatoes, peeled, seeded, and diced (see Note)

1 teaspoon dried oregano

2 bunches broccoli rabe, washed and trimmed

1 teaspoon lemon pepper

Sea salt to taste

Heat the olive oil in a large heavy-bottomed skillet over medium heat. Add the garlic and sauté until lightly browned, about 8 minutes. Add the tomatoes and oregano and cook for about 4 minutes, or until the tomatoes release their juices. Add the broccoli rabe and sauté until crisp-tender and deep green, about 5 minutes. Remove from heat and season with the lemon pepper and sea salt. Serve warm or hot.

• Note: Here's a fast and easy way to peel and skin plum tomatoes: Fill a deep pot with cold water and bring it to a boil. Drop the tomatoes into the boiling water for about 20 seconds. Then remove them with a slotted spoon and plunge into a bowl of cold water. When they are cool enough to handle, slit the skin with a sharp knife. Gently peel the skin off with your fingers; it should loosen and slip off easily.

46

Ground pork tastes best hot off the grill, but these burgers can be broiled in the oven, too. Be creative with your selection of sausage meat. Try spicy, sweet, or seasoned sausages—they all taste great. Sausages seasoned with sun-dried tomatoes, broccoli rabe, or garlic can save prep time and add flavor. Ground pork is a great partner for this sweet and spicy barbecue sauce. This sauce has a rich, intensely sweet taste, so don't make these burgers too big. Serve the burgers on slices of corn bread or if time is short, substitute onion rolls. And, of course, Classic Coleslaw can't be beat.

Grilled Pork Burgers with Molasses Barbecue Sauce

MENU

○ **to eat**

Grilled pork burgers with Molasses barbecue sauce on cornbread or onion rolls

Classic coleslaw

○ **to drink**

Ice cold summer ale or pilsner. Select a light-colored beer that can be quaffed to cool a burning mouth.

serves 4

Grilled Pork Burgers

5 strips thick-cut bacon

2 cloves garlic, crushed

2 small Hungarian wax peppers (also known as banana peppers) or other mild chili peppers, chopped

1 tablespoon ground cumin

1 tablespoon lemon pepper

1/2 pound spicy pork sausages

1/4 pound ground pork

1 tablespoon mayonnaise

Cook the bacon and garlic in a heavy-bottomed skillet over medium heat. When the bacon is about halfway done, add the chopped pepper and sauté until soft, about 4 minutes. Stir in the cumin and lemon pepper and cook for 2 minutes more. Remove from heat and let cool for a few minutes. Pour off, then discard the bacon drippings. Pour the contents of the pan into a food processor fitted with a steel blade and pulse until the bacon and peppers are finely chopped.

Preheat a charcoal or gas grill to medium-high. Split the sausage casings with a knife and crumble contents in a large bowl. Add the ground pork then add half the bacon-pepper mixture and, using your hands or a wooden spoon, mix until the ingredients are evenly distributed. Form into

47

4 burgers of equal size. Grill or broil the burgers, flipping once, brushing the cooked side with 1 tablespoon of the barbecue sauce until the juices run clear, 4 to 5 minutes on each side. While the burgers are cooking, mix the remaining bacon-pepper mixture with the mayonnaise. Serve the burgers on corn bread or onion rolls, topped with the warm Molasses Barbecue Sauce. Serve the Classic Coleslaw on the side.

48

Molasses Barbecue Sauce

3 cups water

2 tablespoons cider vinegar

1/4 cup light unsulphured molasses

1 plum tomato, chopped

3 scallions, white part only, finely chopped

1 clove garlic, minced

1/2 teaspoon crushed red pepper flakes

Combine all the ingredients in a heavy-bottomed saucepan. Bring to a boil, reduce heat to simmer and, stirring periodically to avoid burning. Cook until the quantity is reduced by half, about 15 minutes. Serve warm over the burgers.

Classic Southern Cornbread

1 1/2 cups yellow cornmeal

1/2 cup all-purpose flour

1 tablespoon sugar

2 teaspoons baking powder

1 teaspoon baking soda

1 teaspoon salt

2 large eggs

1 1/2 cups buttermilk

1 cup fresh or frozen corn

Preheat the oven to 425°F. Grease a jelly-roll pan (or shallow metal pan measuring 9 x 12 inches). Into a large bowl, sift together the cornmeal, flour, sugar, baking powder, baking soda, and salt. In a small bowl, beat together the eggs and buttermilk. Pour the buttermilk mixture into the cornmeal mixture and stir in the corn. Stir the batter until just blended, and pour it into the pan, shaking gently to cover the whole pan.

Bake the cornbread for 8 to 10 minutes, or until a tester comes out clean. Allow to cool for about 15 minutes. Cut into 4-inch squares and serve the burgers open-faced on top.

Classic Coleslaw

1/2 cup distilled white vinegar

6 tablespoons sugar

2 teaspoons Dijon mustard

1 teaspoon celery seed (optional)

1/2 large white cabbage (about 4 cups), tough outer leaves discarded, shredded

1 large red onion, thinly sliced

1 large green bell pepper, cored and thinly sliced

Combine the vinegar, sugar, mustard, and celery seeds, if using, in a small saucepan. Stir over low heat until the sugar dissolves. Remove from heat and set aside.

Mix together the cabbage, onion, and green pepper in a large glass bowl. Add the dressing and toss to coat. Cover and refrigerate for at least 2 hours, tossing occasionally. Serve cold.

This burger combines lamb's delicate yet distinctive taste with the Middle Eastern flavor of za'atar, a spice mixture made from sumac, thyme, marjoram, white sesame seeds, and salt. A recipe for this condiment is provided, or you can purchase it from a Middle Eastern store or by mail-order. Its unusual flavor is great on many foods, including meats, grilled vegetables, and poultry, ground or roasted. These burgers are paired with a tabbouleh salad, which also makes a great dip for crudité, a healthful topping for baked potatoes, and a delicious spread for sandwiches.

Grilled Lamb Burgers with Cucumber Yogurt Sauce

MENU

○ **to eat**

Grilled lamb burgers in whole wheat toasted pita pockets

Cucumber yogurt sauce

Za'atar

Classic tabbouleh salad

○ **to drink**

Mango slushie

serves 4

Grilled Lamb Burgers

1 pound ground lamb

1/2 cup dry unseasoned breadcrumbs

1/2 yellow onion, chopped

2 tablespoons za'atar, store-bought or homemade (recipe follows)

2 tablespoons chopped fresh parsley

4 teaspoons minced garlic

1 1/4 teaspoons dried oregano

Sea salt and freshly ground black pepper to taste

Preheat a broiler or charcoal or gas grill to medium-high heat. Using your hands or a wooden spoon, mix together all the ingredients in a large bowl until evenly distributed. Form 4 patties, roughly the same size as small pitas. Broil or grill the burgers, flipping once, until cooked through, about 4 minutes on each side.

Slice open the pita pockets and tuck the burgers inside. Top with the Cucumber Yogurt Sauce, and serve any extra sauce and the Classic Tabbouleh Salad on the side.

49

Cucumber Yogurt Sauce

2 cups plain nonfat or low-fat yogurt

1/4 cup finely chopped red onion

1 medium kirby cucumber, peeled, seeded, and chopped

1 clove garlic, finely chopped

Whisk together all the ingredients in a small glass bowl. Cover and chill for 2 hours before serving.

Za'atar

2 tablespoons toasted white sesame seeds

1/2 cup dried thyme

1/4 cup sumac, available at Middle Eastern grocers or health food stores

1/2 teaspoon sea salt

Preheat the oven to 350°F. Spread the sesame seeds on a small sheet pan or pie plate and toast for 6 minutes. Mix together the toasted sesame seeds, thyme, sumac, and salt. Using a spice mill or mini-chopper, grind the spice mixture into a fine powder. (A mortar and pestle may be used for a rougher finish.) Za'atar may be kept in the refrigerator in a sealed container for 3 to 4 months.

Classic Tabbouleh Salad

1 1/2 cups bulgur (cracked wheat, available at natural food stores and some grocers)

1/2 cup finely chopped parsley

2 scallions, white part and some green, finely chopped

3 ripe plum tomatoes, chopped

3 tablespoons fresh lemon juice

2 tablespoons olive oil

Sea salt and freshly ground black pepper to taste

Place the bulgur in a large bowl and add warm water to cover. Set aside for about 20 minutes, or until the bulgur swells and softens. Drain in a fine-mesh sieve, pressing on the bulgur with a clean dishcloth to remove excess water.

Mix together the parsley, scallions, tomatoes, lemon juice, olive oil, and salt and pepper, tossing to combine. Add the bulgur and mix thoroughly using your hands or a wooden spoon. Serve at room temperature. Leftovers may be kept refrigerated in a sealed container for up to 3 days.

Mango Slushie

2 ripe mangoes, peeled, pitted, and coarsely chopped

2 cups plain low-fat or non-fat yogurt

2 tablespoons fresh lime juice

2 tablespoons sugar

1 cup ice cubes

Place all the ingredients in a blender and blend until smooth, about 1 minute. Add additional ice, if desired, and pour into tall glasses. Serve immediately.

51

For many diners, the idea of fish served any way but as a grilled steak or sautéed fillet brings back dreadful memories of dry salmon croquettes with way too many breadcrumbs or flavorless tuna casseroles. However, fresh fish is more readily available these days, which makes it much easier to prepare fish recipes that taste really good.

Since the following fish burgers don't all call for ground or crumbly fish (the crab cakes and smoked trout burgers are exceptions), perhaps they aren't technically burgers. But if the patties are round and served on a bun with condiments, they get to be called burgers! Of course, if you're a stickler for burger correctness, you could use canned flaked salmon or tuna and they'd look and feel more like burgers, but I strongly recommend that you don't. The flavor and texture of fresh salmon fillets and tuna steaks simply blows the canned stuff out of the water, pun intended. When shopping for fish, look for firm flesh and nice color. The freshest fish has little or no odor. Try to avoid fish packaged in plastic, since it is difficult to ascertain its freshness. Instead buy fish displayed on ice. It's best to buy your fish from a fishmonger instead of going to your local grocery counter. When purchasing crabmeat, shoppers must keep a few things in mind. When it comes to crabcakes, what separates the good from the bad is the origin and freshness of the crabmeat and the amount and type of breading. Lump crabmeat is best: If you can't get to a fish store, then pick up refrigerated or frozen crabmeat from your grocery store fish counter. Avoid canned crabmeat, which tends to be very salty and must be picked over to remove shell bits. ○

While not technically burgers, these **fish** sandwiches are very much at home on a bun. There is no need for special utensils. Besides who really knows what to do with a fish knife!

Angelina's Genuine Maryland Blue Crab Cakes

Angelina's   7135 Harford Road   Baltimore, Maryland   Tel (410) 444-5545

1 pound jumbo lump crabmeat
(preferably fresh and domestic)

1/2 cup unseasoned breadcrumbs

1 teaspoon Old Bay Seasoning

1/2 teaspoon ground white pepper

1/2 tablespoon chopped fresh parsley

2 large eggs, lightly beaten

1 tablespoon mayonnaise

1 teaspoon smooth Dijon mustard

1 teaspoon Worcestershire sauce

3 tablespoons unsalted butter

2 tablespoons dry white wine

1 tablespoon fresh lemon juice

Tartar, cocktail, or Worcestershire sauce,
for serving

54

Crab cakes, once a regional favorite, are available everywhere today, from chain and theme joints to the finest restaurants. We don't call them crab burgers, but they can certainly be served on a bun, flavored with condiments and even garnished with lettuce and tomato if you wish. Preparing them can be tricky, though. Once you begin cooking crab cakes, it may seem almost impossible to keep them from falling apart. The secret is to use enough wet ingredients to bind them together. Panko, or Japanese breadcrumbs, are an excellent alternative to traditional store-bought breadcrumbs. They are lighter and flakier so they won't weigh the cakes down.

This recipe from Angelina's in Baltimore calls for genuine Maryland blue crabmeat. Imported crabmeat is usually processed more than domestic varieties, and you can taste the difference. Angelina's is known for large, fresh crab cakes that taste like crab, not the breading. Fewer breadcrumbs make for more fragile crab cakes, but these are worth the effort.

Put the crabmeat in a large glass bowl, discarding any bits of shell. Pour the breadcrumbs on top of the crabmeat, then add the Old Bay Seasoning, pepper, and parsley on top of the breadcrumbs. Do not mix.

In a separate bowl, whisk together the eggs with the mayonnaise, mustard, and Worcestershire sauce until well blended. Pour the dressing over the crabmeat and mix together very gently with your hands, taking care not to break up the lumps of crab-meat. Form into 4 crab cakes, about 3 inches across and 1 inch thick.

Melt the butter in a large heavy skillet over medium heat. Stir in the wine and lemon juice and bring to a simmer. Add the crab cakes and cook until brown on the outside and cooked through, about 4 minutes on each side. Serve with tartar, cocktail, or Worcestershire sauces on the side.

Wild salmon's popularity has grown in recent years because of a new appreciation of its numerous health benefits including the absence of PCBs often found in farmed salmon. It is high in protein and a rich source of vitamins A and B and Omega-3 oils. The Asian flavors of this fish burger enhance the delicate flavor of the salmon without overwhelming it. Baby bok choy is a leafy green vegetable often found in Asian restaurant dishes. If you can't find it, buy the full-size version and discard the tough outer leaves. In the absence of bok choy, serve braised white or napa cabbage with soy sauce and fresh ginger.

Asian Salmon Burgers

MENU

○ **to eat**

Asian salmon burgers on sesame rolls

Ginger lemon sauce

Baby bok choy salad

○ **to drink**

A Pinot Noir is a favorite with Asian-inspired flavors.

serves 4

Salmon Burgers

1-pound salmon fillet, skin removed, picked over for bones

1 large egg

1 tablespoon low-sodium soy sauce

1 tablespoon minced fresh ginger, minced, or 1/2 teaspoon powdered ginger

1/2 cup panko or other fine unseasoned breadcrumbs

1 teaspoon chopped chives

2 tablespoons red onion, finely chopped

1 tablespoon fresh lemon juice

Sea salt and freshly ground black pepper to taste

Vegetable oil cooking spray

55

Preheat a broiler or charcoal or gas grill to medium heat. Slice the fillet lengthwise into 1/2-inch strips, then cut the strips crosswise to create 1/2-inch cubes.

In a large glass bowl, whisk the egg with the soy sauce and ginger. Add the chopped salmon, panko, chives, onion, and lemon juice, and season with salt and pepper. Using a wooden spoon, mix until the ingredients are evenly distributed. Form into 4 flat patties of equal size. Lightly coat each patty with cooking spray. Broil or grill the burgers, turning them once with care to avoid breaking them, until cooked through, about 5 minutes each side.

Serve on sesame rolls topped with the Ginger Lemon Sauce. Serve extra sauce and the Baby Bok Choy Salad on the side.

Ginger Lemon Sauce

1/4 cup finely chopped red onion

1 clove garlic, minced

1 tablespoon minced fresh ginger, or 1 teaspoon powdered ginger

1 tablespoon fresh lemon juice

1/4 cup low-sodium soy sauce

1/2 teaspoon sugar

Combine all the ingredients in a food processor with a steel blade and pulse until smooth.

Baby Bok Choy Salad

2 tablespoons sesame oil

2 tablespoons finely chopped shallots

2 pounds baby bok choy, trimmed and coarsely chopped

Sea salt and freshly ground black pepper to taste

2 tablespoons toasted sesame seeds

Heat the sesame oil in a large heavy skillet over medium heat. Add the shallots and sauté until they are soft and lightly toasted. Stir in the bok choy and sauté for about 5 minutes more, stirring often, until the green parts have wilted. Reduce heat to low, season with salt and pepper, and toss with the sesame seeds. Serve warm.

Like salmon burgers, tuna burgers should never be made from canned tuna. The flavor of fresh tuna chopped into small dice cannot be duplicated by fish flaked from a can. It just won't taste as good. The stuffed tomatoes are a great accompaniment. For a cocktail party, prepare an hors d'oeuvres platter of herb-stuffed cherry tomatoes and tiny burgers served open-faced on thin white toast.

Big Kahuna Tuna Burgers

MENU

o **to eat**

Big kahuna tuna burgers on whole wheat rolls

Pineapple salsa

Corn- and herb-stuffed tomatoes

Tortilla chips, for the salsa

o **to drink**

Beaujolais-Villages, a popular choice for grilled tuna

serves 4

Tuna Burgers

1 tablespoon vegetable oil

1/4 cup chopped yellow onion

1/4 cup minced red or yellow bell pepper

1-pound tuna steaks, skinned and chopped finely

1 large egg, lightly beaten

1/4 cup Dijon mustard

2 tablespoons chopped fresh parsley

Sea salt and freshly ground black pepper to taste

1/4 cup olive oil

Heat the vegetable oil in a large heavy skillet over medium-high. When the oil is hot but not smoking, sauté the onion and bell pepper until soft and fragrant, about 5 minutes. Transfer to a bowl and set aside.

Using a wooden spoon, mix together the tuna, egg, mustard, and parsley in a large bowl. Season with salt and pepper, add the onion-pepper mixture, and mix again, until ingredients are evenly distributed. Form into 4 patties, cover with plastic wrap, and refrigerate for about 1 hour.

57

Heat the olive oil in the same skillet and pan-fry the burgers, flipping once, until cooked side is lightly browned and crispy, about 4 minutes on each side. Serve on whole wheat rolls and top with the Pineapple Salsa. Serve extra salsa with chips and the Corn- and Herb-Stuffed Tomatoes on the side.

Pineapple Salsa

2 cups chopped fresh or canned pineapple (if using canned, choose unsweetened pineapple and drain well thoroughly)

1/2 cup diced red bell pepper

2 teaspoons fresh lemon juice

1/4 cup chopped scallions, white part only

1 tablespoon chopped fresh cilantro, plus additional sprigs for garnish

1 tablespoon minced fresh ginger, or 1 teaspoon powdered ginger

Mix together all ingredients in a glass bowl. Chill for 1 hour before serving.

Corn- and Herb-Stuffed Tomatoes

4 medium tomatoes (about 1 1/2 pounds), preferably vine-ripened

Sea salt and freshly ground black pepper to taste

4 ears corn (to make 2 cup kernels)

1 red onion, diced

1/4 cup extra-virgin olive oil

2 tablespoons balsamic vinegar

2 tablespoons chopped fresh cilantro

1 teaspoon ground cumin

Core and seed the tomatoes. (One method is to cut a circle the diameter of a half-dollar at the stem end and scoop out the core with a melon baller or grapefruit spoon). Season the insides of the tomatoes with salt and pepper and set aside. Boil the corn until tender, about 5 minutes. Remove the kernels from the corn by standing the wider end of the cob on a cutting board and cutting off the kernels with a sharp knife.

Combine the corn, onion, olive oil, vinegar, cilantro, and cumin, and season with salt and pepper. Mix well and refrigerate for 30 minutes to chill. Stuff the tomatoes with the corn and herb mixture and serve immediately.

Use salmon fillets for these burgers. Burgers made from canned salmon are not worth the effort and may bring back bad memories of school cafeteria salmon croquettes! I recommend using dill Havarti, since dill is frequently paired with salmon and mild enough not to overpower its taste. Succotash, a favorite summer salad, should be made with the freshest corn available. If you are not a lima bean fan, try shelled edamame, Japanese soybeans, in your succotash. They are a great source of protein and delicious, too.

Salmon Burgers with Havarti

MENU

○ **to eat**

Salmon burgers with Havarti on pumpernickel rolls

Dill mayonnaise

Summer succotash

○ **to drink**

A New Zealand Sauvignon Blanc has a clean flavor that works well with salmon.

serves 4

Salmon Burgers

1-pound salmon fillet, skin removed

1/2 cup panko or other unseasoned breadcrumbs

3 tablespoons grated Havarti or dill Havarti

1/4 cup chopped yellow onion

1 teaspoon mustard

2 tablespoons mayonnaise

2 teaspoons chopped fresh dill

Sea salt and freshly ground black pepper to taste

4 thin slices Havarti or dill Havarti

Vegetable oil cooking spray

Preheat a charcoal or gas grill to medium-high heat. Slice the fillet lengthwise into 1-inch strips, then cut the strips crosswise to create 1-inch cubes. In a large glass bowl, mix together the salmon cubes, breadcrumbs, grated cheese, onion, mustard, mayonnaise, and chopped dill, until ingredients are evenly distributed. Season with salt and pepper.

Form 4 patties of equal size and spray them on both sides with cooking spray. Broil or grill the burgers, flipping once when lightly browned and crispy, about 4 minutes on each side. Arrange the slices of cheese

59

on the burgers and place the pumpernickel rolls on the grill rack, cut side down. Close the lid and, if using a gas grill, turn off the heat. Remove after the cheese is melted and the buns are toasted, about 2 minutes. Serve the burgers on the warm rolls, topped with Dill Mayonnaise. Serve the Summer Succotash on the side.

Dill Mayonnaise

3 tablespoons mayonnaise

1 tablespoon Dijon mustard

1 teaspoon chopped fresh dill

Whisk together all the ingredients in a small bowl and serve.

Summer Succotash

1/2 package (8 ounces) frozen shelled edamame (soybeans) or Fordhook lima beans

4 ears fresh corn (to make 2 cups kernels)

3 tablespoons olive oil

2 cloves garlic, minced

2 tablespoons scallions, white part only, minced

1 tablespoon red wine vinegar

2 tablespoons chopped fresh parsley

Sea salt and freshly ground black pepper to taste

Bring a deep pot of water to a boil and add soybeans. Return to a boil and cook for 5 minutes. Remove from heat and drain, then set aside. Remove the kernels from the corn by standing the wider end of the cob on a cutting board and cutting off the kernels with a sharp knife.

Heat 1 tablespoon of the olive oil in a large heavy skillet over medium heat and add the corn, garlic, and scallions. Sauté until the corn is tender, about 4 minutes. Add the edamame, lower the heat, and sauté for about 5 minutes more. Transfer the corn mixture to a large serving bowl. Season with the remaining 2 tablespoons olive oil, vinegar, parsley, and salt and pepper. Serve warm or at room temperature.

Swordfish is one of those foods that evokes memories of warm summer evenings spent cooking dinner on an outdoor grill. However, it would be a sin to chop up a great swordfish steak for burgers. Instead I recommend trimming the steaks to approximate burger shapes. If possible, make the scraps large enough to skewer for kebabs. Just grill the kebabs with a few cherry tomatoes and serve with the Mango Salsa, made from ripe mangoes. The salsa can also be served as a dip for chips.

Tropical Swordfish Burgers

MENU

○ **to eat**

Tropical swordfish burgers on deli rolls with herbed butter

Mango salsa

Tortilla chips for salsa

Grilled leeks

○ **to drink**

Wahine, a 1950s fruit drink that originated at Trader Vic's in Honolulu, Hawaii

serves 4

Swordfish Burgers

2 10-ounce swordfish steaks (about 3/4 inch thick), halved

3 tablespoons fresh lime juice

4 tablespoons low-sodium soy sauce

3 tablespoons olive oil

1 tablespoon minced fresh ginger, or 1 teaspoon powdered ginger

1 clove garlic, mashed

Sea salt and freshly ground black pepper to taste

Trim the swordfish pieces so that they resemble burgers. Whisk together the rest of the ingredients in a large glass bowl. Add the swordfish, tossing to coat it, cover the bowl with plastic wrap, and refrigerate for at least 2 hours.

Preheat a broiler or charcoal or gas grill to medium-high heat. Broil or grill the burgers, flipping once, until the cooked sides are browned, about 4 minutes on each side. Serve on herbed deli rolls and top with Mango Salsa. Serve the extra salsa with chips and the Grilled Leeks on the side.

61

Herbed Butter

4 tablespoons ($1/2$ stick) unsalted butter, softened

1 tablespoon chopped fresh chives, or 2 teaspoons dried chives

1 tablespoons chopped fresh parsley, or 2 teaspoons dried parsley

1 teaspoon lemon pepper

Sea salt

4 deli-style rolls

Mix together the butter, chives, parsley, and lemon pepper, and season with salt. Split the rolls in half and spread with the herbed butter. The butter may be refrigerated for up to 1 week.

Mango Salsa

2 ripe mangoes, peeled and diced

1 Vidalia or other sweet onion, chopped

3 tablespoons chopped fresh cilantro

2 tablespoons freshly squeezed lime juice

Sea salt and freshly ground black pepper to taste

Combine the mangoes, onion, cilantro, and lime juice in a glass bowl. Season with salt and pepper and toss thoroughly. Cover and chill for at least 1 hour before serving. The salsa may be kept refrigerated in a sealed container for up to 3 days.

Grilled Leeks

4 leeks, washed and trimmed

1 large clove garlic

1 tablespoon olive oil

2 tablespoons chopped fresh parsley

Sea salt and freshly ground black pepper to taste

Cut an X in the root end of each leek and soak them in cold water for 10 minutes to remove any remaining grit. Remove all but one of the tough outer leaves. Cut each leek in half lengthwise and tie it back together using the remaining outer leaf.

Preheat a charcoal or gas grill to medium heat. Cut the garlic clove in half and rub the cut side all over the leeks. Tuck the garlic in one of the leek leaves or discard. Brush the leeks with the olive oil, sprinkle with the chopped parsley, and season with salt and pepper. Grill the leeks until the leaves are golden brown but not scorched, about 4 minutes on each side. Serve immediately.

Wahine

1 cup ice cubes

4 cups fresh pineapple juice (or unsweetened store-bought juice)

4 tablespoons fresh lemon juice

$1/4$ cup sugar

$1/2$ cup dark Jamaican rum (optional)

Maraschino cherries and pineapple chunks on skewers

Place the ice in a blender and process until it's crushed. Add the pineapple juice, lemon juice, sugar, and rum, if desired, and blend until smooth. Fill tall glasses with two or three ice cubes and pour the mixture into the glasses. Garnish with the skewered fruit.

These smoked trout burgers might sound a bit unusual, but they have a subtle yet distinctive taste that makes them a wonderful alternative to the bagels with smoked salmon brunch routine. Look for smoked trout in the deli section of your grocery store near the prepared cream cheeses and other varieties of smoked fish. It should be picked over for small bones before cooking. The intensity of the Horseradish Mayonnaise can be heated up or toned down, based on your fellow diners' palates and your own.

Pan-Fried Smoked Trout Burgers

MENU

○ **to eat**

Pan-fried smoked trout burgers on poppy seed rolls

Horseradish mayonnaise

Carrot slaw

Oven-baked potato chips

○ **to drink**

A crisp Chardonnay complements these rich smoky burgers and the slight sweetness of the Carrot Slaw.

serves 4

Trout Burgers

1 1/2 cups smoked trout, broken into small pieces with a fork

1 tablespoon minced shallot

1 tablespoon chopped fresh parsley

1 large egg, lightly beaten

2 tablespoons milk (preferably whole-fat)

1/2 cup panko or other unseasoned breadcrumbs

4 tablespoons (1/2 stick) unsalted butter

Sea salt and freshly ground black pepper to taste

Combine the trout, shallot, and chopped parsley in a large glass bowl, then stir in the beaten egg, milk, and 1/4 cup of the panko with a fork. Gently form the mixture into 4 patties of equal size, then dip them in the remaining 1/4 cup panko, pressing down gently so the breadcrumbs stick.

Heat the butter in large heavy skillet over medium heat. Pan-fry the burgers, flipping once, until golden brown and cooked through, about 4 minutes on each side. Serve on poppy seed rolls topped with the Horseradish Mayonnaise. Serve the Carrot Slaw and Oven-baked Potato Chips on the side.

63

Horseradish Mayonnaise

3 tablespoons mayonnaise

1 tablespoon Dijon mustard

1 tablespoon prepared white horseradish, or 1 teaspoon grated fresh horseradish

Whisk together all the ingredients in a glass bowl. Chill until serving time.

Carrot Slaw

1 small head purple cabbage, outer leaves discarded, grated

2 large carrots, grated

2 tablespoons chopped fresh cilantro

2 tablespoons red wine vinegar

1/4 cup extra-virgin olive oil

2 teaspoons sugar

1 teaspoon cumin

Sea salt and freshly ground black pepper to taste

Combine the cabbage, carrots, and cilantro in a glass bowl. In a separate bowl, whisk the vinegar with the olive oil, sugar, cumin, and salt and pepper. Pour the dressing over the shredded vegetables and toss to combine. Chill for 1 hour before serving.

Oven-baked Potato Chips

6 tablespoons vegetable oil

3 Idaho potatoes (about 1 1/2 pounds)

2 tablespoons fresh chives, finely chopped

Salt to taste

Grease 2 large baking sheets well with 1 tablespoon of the vegetable oil. Preheat the oven to 400°F. Peel the potatoes and slice them into very thin slices. Place the potato slices in a large bowl, add the oil, and toss well, being sure to separate the slices. Place the slices on greased baking sheets in a single layer.

Bake the potatoes in middle of oven until golden, 12 to 15 minutes. Remove from oven and transfer to a bowl or basket lined with paper towels. Sprinkle with the chives, and salt. Serve warm. Leftovers may be stored in an airtight container for up to 3 days.

65

If a burger doesn't contain meat is it still a burger? You bet it is! If it includes a tasty patty that sits on a piece of bread and has a "lid," it counts. With legions of Americans eschewing meat for a variety of reasons, vegetable, grain, and bean burgers have become increasingly popular. Some of the recipes that follow, like the Falafel in a Pita Pocket, have been favorites for years, here and abroad. Others, like the Tofu Burgers with Peanut Sauce and the Feijoada Black Bean Burgers, are new twists on familiar ingredients or traditional dishes.

Although fresh veggie burgers are often considered whole food restaurant fare, they are simpler to make than you might think. The trick is to make patties that hold together without getting gummy. The secret is the right amount of moisture and gentle handling. Vegetable oil cooking spray is a big help; not only can you spray it on the grill rack or pan, you can spray it on the burgers and on your hands when forming patties.

Even if you are a devoted carnivore, bear in mind that most veggie burgers pack a nutritional whallop unlikely to be found in a burger made with meat. Homemade veggie and grain burgers also don't contain binders or texturizers, the strangely unfamiliar stuff in commercially prepared ones. ○

Falafel with Herbed Cucumber Yogurt *p69*

Homemade **vegetarian** burgers made with vegetables or grains offer a delicious way to add fiber and nutrients not found in meat, reduce the fat content, and offer a lower sodium option than store-bought veggie burgers.

Three-Grain Vegetable Burgers

Josie's   565 Third Avenue   New York, New York   Tel (212) 490-1558

- 1/2 cup cooked couscous
- 1/4 cup cooked bulgur (cracked wheat)
- 1/4 cup cooked quinoa
- 1 clove garlic, minced
- 1 tablespoon minced shallots
- 2 tablespoons olive oil
- 2 tablespoons sliced button mushrooms
- 1 tablespoon balsamic vinegar
- 1/4 cup cooked chickpeas
- 1/4 cup minced yellow onions
- 1/4 cup minced carrots
- 1 1/2 tablespoons minced fresh herbs (preferably a combination of parsley, oregano, and tarragon)
- 1 egg white
- 1/2 cup whole wheat breadcrumbs
- Salt and freshly ground black pepper to taste
- Vegetable oil cooking spray

This hearty veggie burger is adapted from a recipe by Louie Lanza, Executive Chef at several New York restaurants including Josie's, Citrus, and Better Burger. It is completely dairy-free. Unlike many vegetable burgers, it is not bound together with cheese, nor does it contain egg yolks, a common allergen. The three grains—couscous, bulgur, and quinoa—may be found at natural food stores and many supermarkets. However, as with all the recipes in this book, the ingredients may be tweaked according to what vegetables and grains you have on hand. A side dish of lightly salted edamame (Japanese soybeans) would be a good accompaniment. In summer, serve with a salad of beefsteak tomatoes, sweet Vidalia onion, fresh basil, and olive oil seasoned with salt and pepper.

Combine the couscous, bulgur, and quinoa in a large bowl and set aside. In a nonstick skillet over medium heat, sauté the garlic and shallots in 1 tablespoon of the olive oil, stirring until golden, about 1 minute. Add the mushrooms and sauté until tender, about 5 minutes more. Stir in the vinegar and cook for a few more minutes. Add the chickpeas and cook until heated through. Pour the sautéed vegetables into a food processor fitted with a steel blade and pulse until smooth. Transfer the puree to a bowl and set aside.

In the same nonstick skillet over medium heat, sauté the onions and carrots in the remaining 1 tablespoon olive oil, stirring until softened, about 5 minutes. Add the vegetable puree and the sautéed onion-carrot mixture to the bowl containing the grains.

Add the fresh herbs, egg white, and breadcrumbs and, using your hands or a wooden spoon, mix well to evenly distribute the ingredients. Season with salt and pepper. Form into 4 patties of equal size, flattening them slightly with your hand. Cover tightly with plastic wrap and refrigerate for at least 2 hours. Grease a nonstick skillet with cooking spray and set the pan over medium heat. Pan-fry the burgers until lightly browned, pressing them flat with a spatula several times, about 4 minutes on each side. Serve immediately.

68

Falafel is a Middle Eastern specialty that is quite simple to prepare. You simply fry small patties of ground chickpeas. Some recipes include other types of beans, but I prefer falafel made with chickpeas only. When garnished with a cool yogurt cucumber sauce, this meal will appeal to even the most devoted meat-and-potatoes souls. Couscous is a natural accompaniment for falafel, but a pasta salad made with orzo or another small noodle would be nice, too. Toss the chilled pasta with corn, cilantro, and a warm red wine vinaigrette.

Falafel with Herbed Cucumber Yogurt

MENU

○ **to eat**

Falafel with herbed cucumber yogurt in pita pockets

Shredded lettuce, tomato, and red onion garnish

Couscous with pine nuts and apricots

○ **to drink**

Desert fruit cooler

serves 4

Falafel

4 scallions, cut into 1-inch pieces

2 cloves garlic, halved

$1/2$ cup coarsely chopped fresh cilantro

$1/4$ cup coarsely chopped fresh mint

One 15-ounce can chickpeas, rinsed and drained

$1/2$ cup plain dried breadcrumbs

1 teaspoon ground cumin

1 teaspoon baking powder

$1/2$ teaspoon sea salt

1 teaspoon Tabasco sauce

Vegetable oil cooking spray

2 tablespoons olive oil

69

In food processor fitted with a steel blade, combine the scallions, garlic, cilantro, and mint, and pulse until finely chopped. Add the chickpeas, breadcrumbs, cumin, baking powder, salt, and Tabasco and continue to pulse until the batter has the consistency of cooked oatmeal. Lightly oil your hands and form 4 burger-shaped patties. Lightly spray the patties with cooking spray on both sides.

Heat the olive oil in large nonstick skillet over medium heat until it's hot but not smoking. Pan-fry the falafel, flipping once, until golden brown and crisp, about 4 minutes on each side. Drain the cooked falafel on a plate lined with paper towels. Serve warm, in pita pockets garnished with shredded lettuce, chopped tomatoes, and sliced onions. Top with Herbed Cucumber Yogurt and serve Couscous with Pine Nuts and Apricots on the side.

Herbed Cucumber Yogurt

1 cup plain low-fat or fat-free yogurt

1 clove garlic, minced

2 tablespoons fresh lemon juice

1 kirby cucumber or 1/2 English cucumber, seeded and chopped

Sea salt and freshly ground black pepper to taste

Whisk together all the ingredients in a small glass bowl. Cover and chill until serving time.

Couscous with Pine Nuts and Apricots

1 tablespoon olive oil

1/4 cup finely chopped shallots

2 cups low-sodium vegetable broth

1 cup chopped dried apricots

One 10-ounce package couscous

1/2 cup toasted pine nuts (toast on a small baking sheet in a 350°F oven for 10 minutes)

Sea salt and freshly ground black pepper to taste

Heat the olive oil in a small saucepan over medium heat. Add the shallots and sauté until golden, about 4 minutes. Remove from heat and set aside.

In a heavy-bottomed pot, bring the vegetable broth and apricots to a boil. Stir in the couscous, cover the pot, and remove from heat. Let sit for about 5 minutes, then add the sautéed shallots, toasted pine nuts, and salt and pepper. Fluff the couscous mixture with a fork to break up any lumps. Serve warm alongside the falafel burgers, or serve the falafel on a bed of the couscous.

Desert Fruit Cooler

2 cups cold water

1 cup ice cubes

2 cups mixed summer fruit (honeydew melon, cantaloupe, mango, watermelon, papaya, strawberries, and raspberries), coarsely chopped if necessary

1/4 cup sugar

1 tablespoon fresh lime juice, or more to taste

Combine all the ingredients in a blender and blend until smooth. Strain the fruit mixture through a fine-mesh sieve into a large glass pitcher. Stir before serving in tall glasses over ice.

For many of us, the word tofu evokes Birkenstocks, communal living, and mushy textures. But don't underrate it; its increasing popularity at restaurants is a testament to its nutritional merits and versatility. Much like cow's milk that is separated to form cheese, the soy milk, or liquid extracted from soybeans, is separated into curds and whey to form tofu. Like potatoes, tofu can be baked, fried, broiled, and roasted, but unlike potatoes, it is full of totally digestible protein and has more nutritional bang for the bite than almost any other food. Try this recipe for tofu burgers and see how it will become a regular part of your burger repertoire.

Thai-Flavored Tofu Burgers with Nuts

MENU

o **to eat**

Thai-flavored tofu burgers with nuts on sesame seed rolls

Peanut sauce

Confetti rice salad

Vegetable crudité and pita chips

o **to drink**

Honey soy shake

serves 4

Tofu Burgers

One 12-ounce package firm tofu, drained and cut in half

2 tablespoons peanut oil

1/2 cup grated carrot

1/2 teaspoon chopped lemon grass

1/2 cup thinly sliced scallions (both green and white parts)

1 clove garlic, minced

1 tablespoon finely chopped fresh ginger, or 1 teaspoon ground ginger

1/2 cup chopped peanuts

2 tablespoons soy sauce

Sea salt and freshly ground black pepper to taste

To remove excess moisture from the tofu, wrap it in several layers of paper towels, place it on a large plate, and top with a heavy book for 30 minutes to 1 hour. Press down on the tofu to squeeze out as much moisture as possible, then discard the paper towels. Transfer the tofu to a large glass bowl and crumble it with your fingers.

Preheat the broiler. Lightly grease a broiling pan with 1 tablespoon of the peanut oil. Heat the remaining 1 tablespoon peanut oil in a heavy skillet over medium heat. Add the carrots, lemon grass, scallions, garlic, and ginger and sauté until fragrant and soft, about 5 minutes. Add the sautéed vegetables to the tofu, then add the peanuts and soy sauce, mixing well to evenly distribute the ingredients. Season with salt and pepper. Form the tofu mixture into 4 patties of equal size. Broil the burgers, flipping once, until heated through, about 4 minutes on each side. Serve on sesame seed buns, topped with peanut sauce. Serve the Confetti Rice Salad and the extra Peanut Sauce with crudité and pita chips on the side.

Peanut Sauce

1 cup creamy peanut butter

1 cup vegetable stock

1 tablespoon brown sugar

1 tablespoon low-sodium soy sauce

Combine all the ingredients in a small saucepan. Simmer over low heat until the peanut butter is melted and smooth. Remove from heat and let cool for about 30 minutes before serving.

Confetti Rice Salad

1/2 cup plus 1 tablespoon extra-virgin olive oil

1 yellow bell pepper, diced

1 red bell pepper, diced

1 green bell pepper, diced

4 scallions, white part only, chopped

10 grape or cherry tomatoes, cut in half

2 cups brown rice, cooked according to package directions

2 tablespoons red wine vinegar

1 clove garlic, minced

Sea salt and freshly ground black pepper to taste

Heat 1 tablespoon of the olive oil in a heavy skillet over medium heat. Add the peppers, scallions, and tomatoes and sauté, stirring until soft and fragrant, about 5 minutes. Add the cooked rice and reduce heat to low. Whisk together the vinegar, garlic, and remaining 1/2 cup olive oil. Pour over the rice and vegetable mixture and remove from heat. Transfer to a serving bowl, season with salt and pepper, and serve warm or at room temperature.

Honey Soy Shake

2 bananas, peeled and broken into pieces

2 cups soy milk

2 cups ice cubes

2 tablespoons honey

1 teaspoon almond extract

Place all the ingredients in a blender and process until smooth. Pour into tall glasses and serve immediately.

Black beans are familiar to most of us as sauces for Chinese take-out and as side dishes for tacos and enchiladas. Since they are nutritionally full of good things and readily take on the flavor of whatever spices you use, I've created a recipe I hope you'll find pleasantly surprising. This recipe is a twist on feijoada, the national dish of Brazil, usually a platter of pork sausages and sliced meats accompanied by black beans and other side dishes. These feijoada burgers however are made with sweet potatoes and contain no meat but are accented with the same spices as the original dish. They have a meaty texture that will fill you up just like a good beef burger.

Feijoada Black Bean Burgers

MENU

o to eat

Feijoada black bean burgers on multigrain buns

Chili mayonnaise

Fresh corn fritters

o to drink

A chilled Zinfandel makes a cool and refreshing accompaniment.

serves 4

Black Bean Burgers

1 large sweet potato

2 tablespoons olive oil

1 red bell pepper, cored and chopped

2 cloves garlic, minced

1 large Spanish onion, chopped

1 large tomato, chopped

1 tablespoon ground cumin

1 teaspoon crushed red pepper flakes

1 teaspoon ground cardamom

1 bay leaf

3 cups cooked black beans, drained and rinsed

1 teaspoon sea salt

Freshly ground black pepper to taste

Preheat the oven to 425°F. Scrub the sweet potato, pat dry, and poke 5 or 6 times with a fork. Bake until tender, about 1 hour. Let cool for about 15 minutes, until it can be easily handled. Remove the skin and gently crumble the flesh into a large bowl.

While the potato is baking, heat the olive oil in a heavy-bottomed pot over medium heat. Add the bell pepper, garlic, onion, tomato, cumin, red pepper flakes, cardamom, and bay leaf. Cook until the peppers are soft, the onion is translucent, and the tomatoes release their juices, about 8 to 10 minutes. Remove from heat,

73

Chili Mayonnaise

1 cup mayonnaise

1 tablespoon orange juice

1 teaspoon chili powder

Sea salt and freshly ground black pepper to taste

Whisk together all the ingredients in a small glass bowl. Cover and chill until serving time.

Fresh Corn Fritters

4 ears corn (to make 2 cup kernels)

2 tablespoons all-purpose flour, or more if needed

2 large eggs, lightly beaten

1 teaspoon baking powder

Vegetable oil cooking spray

Sea salt to taste

stir in the black beans, and set aside to cool. Drain juices from pan and reserve. Remove bay leaf.

Preheat a broiler or charcoal or gas grill to medium heat. Add the pepper-bean mixture to the cooled potatoes and season with the salt and pepper. Using your hands, mix until the ingredients are evenly incorporated. Form 4 patties of equal size and lightly brush them with olive oil. Broil or grill the burgers, flipping once, until they are crisp on the outside, about 4 minutes on each side. Serve on multigrain buns topped with Chili Mayonnaise. Serve the extra Chili Mayonnaise and Fresh Corn Fritters on the side.

Mix together the corn, flour, eggs, and baking powder. Oil a large nonstick skillet with nonstick cooking spray and set over medium heat. Using a table-spoon, spoon the batter onto the skillet to form fritters slightly larger than half-dollars. If the fritters are too loose add a teaspoon of flour to firm the batter. Pan-fry until brown and crisp, about 4 minutes on each side. Transfer the cooked fritters to a plate lined with paper towels to drain. Sprinkle with salt, and serve warm.

When veggie burgers are bad, they are mealy and flavorless, but when they are good, they are crisp, colorful, and taste like summer. I believe the secret to a really great veggie burger is using fresh vegetables and taking care not to over-cook them. Don't be afraid to experiment with this recipe: If there's a vegetable you can't stand, substitute one you like better. This burger is accompanied with a pasta salad that is great warm or cold. For a warming winter meal, try serving these veggie burgers on a bed of warm pasta, minus the bun.

Southwestern Veggie Burgers

MENU

○ **to eat**

Southwestern veggie burgers on Bruschetta bread

Simple salsa

Pasta salad with garlic and sun-dried tomatoes

○ **to drink**

Strawberry lemonade

serves 4

Veggie Burgers

3 ears fresh corn (to yield 1 1/2 cups corn kernels)

1/2 red onion, coarsely chopped

1/2 red pepper, coarsely chopped

1/2 cup broccoli florets

10 small button mushrooms

1/2 cup dry unseasoned breadcrumbs

2 tablespoons vegetable stock

1/4 cup chopped fresh cilantro

1 teaspoon crushed red pepper flakes

1 large egg, lightly beaten

Sea salt and freshly ground black pepper to taste

Vegetable oil cooking spray

75

Combine all of the ingredients (except the cooking spray) in a food processor fitted with a steel blade. Pulse until the mixture thickens and has the consistency of cooked oatmeal. Lightly oil your hands with cooking spray and form the mixture into 4 patties of equal size.

Preheat a broiler or charcoal or gas grill to medium heat. Spray both sides of the patties with cooking spray. Broil or grill the burgers, flipping once, until they are crisp and medium brown on the outside, about 4 minutes on each side. Serve on bruschetta bread topped with the Simple Salsa. Serve with extra Simple Salsa as a condiment and the Pasta Salad with Garlic and Sun-dried Tomatoes on the side.

Simple Salsa

3 ripe plum tomatoes, coarsely chopped

1 small onion, coarsely chopped

1 clove garlic, minced

2 tablespoons chopped fresh cilantro

1 teaspoon grated lime zest

1 teaspoon hot pepper sauce

1 teaspoon olive oil

Sea salt and freshly ground black pepper to taste

Mix together all the ingredients in a glass bowl. Cover and chill until serving time.

Bruschetta Bread

1 tablespoon olive oil

2 tablespoons Simple Salsa

8 slices Italian bread, about $1/2$ inch thick

Mix the olive oil with the salsa in a small bowl. Spread on one side of each slice of bread, and place under broiler for about 1 minute. Serve with the Southwestern Veggie Burgers.

Pasta Salad with Garlic and Sun-dried Tomatoes

6 cloves garlic

$1/2$ pound rotini or small penne

$1/2$ cup sun-dried tomatoes packed in oil, drained and finely chopped

2 tablespoons olive oil

Sea salt and freshly ground black pepper to taste

Freshly grated Parmigiano-Reggiano

Preheat the oven to 400°F. Wrap the unpeeled garlic cloves in aluminum foil and bake until soft, about 45 minutes. While the garlic is roasting, cook the pasta according to package instructions. When the pasta is al dente, drain in a colander and return to the pot. Squeeze the roasted garlic pulp from the skins and mash with the flat side of a large knife. Add the garlic and sun-dried tomatoes to the pasta, toss with the olive oil, and season with salt and pepper. Sprinkle with the cheese and serve warm.

Strawberry Lemonade

2 cups strawberries, stems removed, cut in half

1 $1/2$ cups fresh lemon juice

1 $1/2$ cups sugar, or more to taste

4 cups cold water

Combine the strawberries and $1/4$ cup of the lemon juice in a blender and blend until smooth. Strain through a wire-mesh sieve into a large glass pitcher. Add the remaining 1 $1/4$ cup lemon juice, sugar, and water and stir until the sugar is dissolved. Taste and add more sugar if the strawberries were not very sweet. Serve in tall glasses over ice.

• Note: This drink is a delicious way to enjoy ripe strawberries. It can be spiked with a little vodka or rum or served as is over ice.

76

Once considered the poor relation of fancier mushrooms, the Portobello has grown in popularity. Its meaty texture and woody flavor were found to be a nice substitute for animal protein. The stems of these mushrooms are too tough for this recipe, but you can add them chopped to a veggie burger. Three-Pepper Slaw has become a replacement for coleslaw in my house. Its color, flavor, and fridge life are perfect during summer when red, yellow, and orange peppers are plentiful at the green grocer, or if you are lucky enough, in your own garden!

Portobello Mushroom Burgers

MENU

○ **to eat**

Portobello mushroom burgers on onion rolls

Red pepper hummus

Three-pepper slaw

○ **to drink**

Pair with a Chilean Merlot, the South American wine of the moment.

serves 4

Mushroom Burgers

$1/2$ cup good-quality olive oil

2 cloves garlic, minced

1 tablespoon chopped red onion

1 tablespoon chopped fresh basil

Sea salt and freshly ground black pepper to taste

4 large Portobello mushrooms, wiped of dirt with a damp paper towel, stems removed

Heat the olive oil in a small sauté pan over medium heat. Add the garlic and onion and sauté until fragrant and softened, about 6 minutes. Set aside to cool.

Preheat a broiler or charcoal or gas grill to medium-high heat. Whisk the basil into the garlic and oil mixture and season with salt and pepper. Brush liberally over the tops and bottoms of the mushroom to thoroughly coat. Grill the mushrooms for 4 minutes on each side, brushing additional olive oil mixture on the cooked side if desired.

Serve the mushrooms on onion rolls topped with the Red Pepper Hummus. Serve extra hummus and the Three-Pepper Slaw on the side.

Red Pepper Hummus

2 red bell peppers, roasted and peeled
(prepared may be used)

1/2 cup chopped fresh cilantro

1 clove garlic

One 15-ounce can chickpeas,
drained and rinsed

2 tablespoons sesame tahini

1 tablespoon fresh lemon juice

1 teaspoon ground cumin

1 tablespoon extra-virgin olive oil

Sea salt and freshly ground black pepper

Place all the ingredients in a food
processor fitted with a steel blade
and pulse for about 30 seconds,
or until smooth. Scrape down the
sides of the work bowl with a rubber
spatula and pulse again. Season
with salt and pepper. Chill for about
1 hour before serving. Red Pepper
Hummus may be refrigerated in a
sealed container for up to 1 week.

Three-Pepper Slaw

2 tablespoons mayonnaise

1 clove garlic, minced

1 teaspoon ground cumin

1/4 cup chopped onion

Sea salt and freshly ground black
pepper to taste

3 bell peppers (red, orange, and yellow),
cut into very thin strips

1 tablespoon chopped fresh cilantro

Whisk the mayonnaise with the
garlic, cumin, and onion, and
season with salt and pepper.
Combine the julienned peppers
in a large serving bowl, add the
dressing, and toss to coat. Chill at
least 1 hour. Just before serving,
stir in the chopped cilantro.

79

If you have kids, you have dealt with that plaintive mealtime wail . . . "I hate this." When you point out to your child that she or he has eaten turkey from the deli a million times and this is turkey, too, it is met with even more resistance. Don't despair . . . there is life beyond mac and cheese and hot dogs.

The secret to serving your kids a diverse menu is giving them the familiar with a twist. Expand their horizons just a bit at a time, not all in one meal. If they love fried chicken fingers, try a baked chicken burger on a familiar bun. If they love cheese, give them a cheeseburger made with ground turkey or chicken. If they dig pizza, serve a pizza burger made from the other white meat: pork.

These side dishes have been enthusiastically consumed by some of the most finicky eaters in the Western Hemisphere. Some, like homemade potato chips may seen labor intensive when there's a perfectly good bag of chips in the pantry. But these will taste crispier, are lower in salt, and are actually made from potatoes.

Also included are some delicious, nutritious drinks that will certainly be welcome alternatives to milk and juice. Letting your little ones help make this part of the meal will earn you all kinds of good will at the dinner table! ○

Happily, most kids will readily eat a burger, so slip one of these **kid-friendly** alternatives into a bun and pull a fast one on your kids. And while you are at it, sneak a vegetable on the plate.

Four Cheese Burgers *p83*

The Wind-Chill Factory Burger
with Michigan Sauce

**The Wind-Chill Factory Restaurant   Route 9N and Alexandria Avenue   Ticonderoga, New York
Tel (518) 585-3044   *(open from April 1 through Columbus Day)***

1 tablespoon olive oil

2 tablespoons yellow onion, chopped

1/4 cup white vinegar

1 tablespoon brown sugar

1 tablespoon yellow mustard

1 tablespoon Worcestershire sauce

4 teaspoon cayenne pepper

1 teaspoon chili powder

1 tablespoon honey

1 small can tomato paste

1 pound ground top round

82

The burger from The Wind-Chill Factory Restaurant in Ticonderoga, New York is the stuff of local legend. Fashioned after the old-style drive-in burger spot, this culinary throwback supplies hordes of hungry visitors, native and not, with rib-sticking grub and great ice cream. Kids love their burgers and hot dogs generously coated with what's known in the Champlain region as Michigan sauce. There is no known reason for the sauce bearing the name of a state quite a distance away and the subject has been the source of some confusion amongst visitors from the Great Lakes State. Whatever its provenance, it is delicious. It bears a resemblance to barbecue sauce but has a slightly sharper flavor and seems to strike the perfect balance between sweet and spicy. Owner Robert Porter says patrons often ask for extra sauce as a dip for one of the many types of fries available, as sauce for a hot pretzel, and as a hot dog topping. It seems most at home, however, on a burger and if you feel that you can't get enough of it on top of your burger, try mixing in a teaspoon or two into the ground beef before cooking. Onions may be omitted for the onion-phobic child. This sauce can also be used as a base for a "sloppy joe" style sandwich. Just sauté the ground beef in a separate pan, drain and add to the simmering sauce. Serve burgers or sloppy joes on your favorite buns or rolls.

To prepare the Michigan sauce, heat olive oil in a saucepan over medium heat. Saute the onion until soft and translucent. Turn burner to low and stir in the vinegar, brown sugar, mustard, Worcestershire sauce, cayenne, chili powder, and honey. Simmer over low heat for 10 minutes, then stir in the tomato paste.

Simmer for 5 more minutes and remove from heat.

Preheat grill or broiler. Form 4 burgers and cook 4 minutes on each side or until cooked through. Place burger on bottom bun half and top with a heaping tablespoon of Michigan sauce. Top with bun and serve.

Cheeseburgers, traditionally made with cheese on top, are just as good when the cheese is grated or cubed and added to the ground meat. My son Charlie loves cheese, so these burgers are his way to get as many cheeses into one meal as possible. Be creative and try different types of cheese: Charlie loves cheddar, Colby, Muenster, and smoked cheeses, too. Homemade potato chips are the perfect accompaniment. They are a breeze to make if your food processor has a slicing blade, or you can use a mandoline or a large grater with a slicing surface. Yukon Golds make great chips.

Four-Cheese Burgers

MENU

○ **to eat**

Four-cheese burgers on Cheesy corn rolls

Homemade potato chips

Creamy green and yellow veggies

○ **to drink**

Berry berry iced tea

serves 4

Four-Cheese Burgers

1 pound ground chuck

1 Vidalia or other sweet onion, chopped

1 tablespoon Worcestershire sauce

2 tablespoons grated sharp cheddar

2 tablespoons grated Monterey Jack

2 tablespoons grated Colby

1 thick slice mozzarella, quartered

Sea salt and freshly ground black pepper to taste

Vegetable oil cooking spray

Preheat the broiler or a charcoal or gas grill to medium high. Combine the ground meat, onion, Worcestershire sauce, and the grated cheeses, mixing with your hands so that the ingredients are evenly distributed. Form 8 very thin patties of equal size. Top 4 of the patties with the mozzarella pieces and top those with the other 4 patties. Press the edges to seal in the mozzarella, then lightly spray the burgers with cooking spray. Grill the burgers until cooked through, about 5 minutes each side. Serve on the warm Cheesy Corn Rolls with Homemade Potato Chips and Creamy Green and Yellow Veggies on the side.

83

Cheesy Corn Rolls

Vegetable oil cooking spray

1/2 cup cornmeal

1/2 cup all-purpose flour

1 teaspoon baking powder

Sea salt to taste

1/2 cup milk (fat-free is fine)

1/2 cup grated sharp cheddar

1 large egg

2 teaspoons unsalted butter, melted

Preheat the oven to 400°F. Lightly grease a 9-inch square baking pan with cooking spray and set aside. In a medium bowl, mix the cornmeal, flour, baking powder, and salt. Add the milk, cheese, egg, and melted butter and stir until the dry ingredients are moist. Pour the batter into the greased pan and bake until the top is golden brown and spongy to the touch, about 20 minutes. Cool in the pan for about 10 minutes. Using a large mouthed glass or mug or cookie cutter, form 8 round "buns." Serve warm.

Homemade Potato Chips

3 Idaho baking potatoes
(about 1 1/2 pounds)

1/2 cup canola oil

Sea salt to taste

Preheat the oven to 400°F. Peel the potatoes and drop them into a large bowl of cold water and ice to prevent discoloration. Pat the potatoes dry with paper towels. In a food processor fitted with a slicing disk, very thinly slice the potatoes. Alternately, use a sharp knife to very thinly slice the potatoes, returning them to the cold water until they're ready to use. Drain potatoes in a colander and pat dry with paper towels.

Return the potato slices to the bowl and toss with the canola oil, separating the slices so that both sides are coated with the oil. Arrange the slices on a baking sheet in a single layer. (You may have to cook the chips in batches.) Bake the chips until they are golden and the edges begin to curl slightly. Lightly salt the chips and serve warm.

Creamy Green and Yellow Veggies

3 cups sugar snap peas, strings removed

2 cups fresh or frozen corn

1/4 cup heavy cream

Sea salt and freshly ground black pepper to taste

Boil 1 quart water in a large pot, add the snap peas, and return to a boil. Cook for about 1 minute, then remove the peas with a slotted spoon and drop them into a bowl of cold water to stop the cooking. Bring the water to a boil again, add the corn and return to a boil. Cook the corn for about 3 minutes, then remove it with tongs. When the corn is cool enough to handle, cut off the kernels from the cobs with a sharp knife.

Heat the cream in a saucepan until it boils. Lower the heat, add the peas and corn, and toss to combine. Season with salt and pepper and toss again. Serve warm.

Berry Berry Iced Tea

3 decaffeinated tea bags

3 berry-flavored tea bags

6 cups boiling water

3 tablespoons sugar

1 tablespoon fresh lemon juice

Remove the paper tags and staples from the teabag strings and tie all the strings together. Place the tea bags in a large pitcher and pour the boiling water over them. Stir in the sugar and allow the tea to steep for 1 hour, until it has cooled to room temperature. Remove the teabags, squeezing out any excess tea. Stir in the lemon juice and serve in glasses filled with ice.

There was a time not too long ago when we couldn't dine out as a family unless the menu had chicken fingers. Well, after a few too many of those meals, I set out to find a version that was a little less greasy and a lot more appetizing. By baking a few vegetables alongside the chicken breasts, you can save a little time. Cheesy Zucchini Boats are meant to encourage your kids' consumption of fresh vegetables and have been well received in my house. Experiment with the fillings: You can try rice, beans, nuts, and even seasoned breadcrumbs with a little steamed broccoli or grated carrot.

Peanut Chicken Burgers with Peanut Sauce

MENU

○ **to eat**

Peanut chicken burgers with Peanut sauce in whole wheat pita pockets

Cheesy zucchini boats

Roasted new potatoes

○ **to drink**

Peanut butter milkshakes

serves 4

Chicken Burgers

3 boneless skinless chicken breast halves, trimmed of fat

2 large eggs, lightly beaten

1 cup unseasoned breadcrumbs

$1/2$ cup unsalted peanuts, finely chopped

$1/2$ teaspoon paprika

$1/2$ teaspoon garlic powder

$1/2$ teaspoon cumin

Sea salt and freshly ground black pepper to taste

Vegetable oil cooking spray

Preheat the oven to 350°F. Cut the chicken into 1-inch pieces. Combine the beaten eggs and chunks of chicken in a bowl and toss to coat. In another bowl, combine the bread-crumbs, chopped peanuts, paprika, garlic powder, cumin, and salt and pepper. Using a slotted spoon, remove the chicken from the egg mixture and add to the breadcrumb mixture. Using your hands, mix until the ingredients are evenly distributed. Form 4 patties of equal size.

85

Coat a baking sheet with nonstick cooking spray and arrange the burgers on the pan so they don't touch. Bake until the patties are firm and brown on top, about 30 minutes. Serve the burgers in whole wheat pitas topped with the Peanut Sauce. Serve extra sauce on the side.

Peanut Sauce

1/2 cup chunky peanut butter

5 tablespoons low-sodium chicken stock, or more if necessary to thin

1 tablespoon brown sugar

1 tablespoon low-sodium soy sauce

Heat the peanut butter in a small saucepan over low heat. When the peanut butter has begun to melt, slowly stir in the chicken stock, brown sugar, and soy sauce. When the sauce begins to thicken, after about 10 minutes, remove from heat. If the sauce is too thick, thin it with additional chicken stock.

Cheesy Zucchini Boats

2 medium zucchini

2 tablespoons unsalted butter

2 cups cooked brown rice

9 tablespoons grated Parmesan

Sea salt and freshly ground black pepper to taste

Preheat the oven to 350°F. Cut the zucchini in half lengthwise. Scoop out the seeds and pulp and set aside. (Be careful not to pierce the skins as you scoop.) Arrange the zucchini shells, cut side down, in a large baking dish. Add about 2 cups water. Bake until the skins are slightly soft, about 15 minutes.

While the zucchini shells are baking, coarsely chop the zucchini pulp. Melt the butter in a skillet, add the chopped zucchini, and cook over low heat until soft. Stir in the cooked rice and reheat for a minute or two. Remove from heat, add 3 tablespoons of the cheese, and stir again. Season the rice stuffing with salt and pepper.

Carefully fill the baked zucchini shells with the stuffing, sprinkle with the remaining cheese, and bake until the cheese is lightly browned, about 15 minutes.

Roasted New Potatoes

2 pounds small red-skinned potatoes, cut into quarters

2 tablespoons olive oil

2 tablespoons chopped fresh parsley

1 tablespoon chopped fresh rosemary, or 1 teaspoon dried rosemary

Sea salt and freshly ground black pepper to taste

3 garlic cloves, unpeeled

Toss the potatoes with the olive oil until thoroughly coated. Add the parsley, rosemary, and salt and pepper, and toss again.

Preheat the oven to 350°F. Arrange the potatoes and garlic on a baking sheet in a single layer. Bake until the potatoes are tender and slightly browned, about 30 minutes. Transfer the potatoes to a serving bowl. Squeeze the pulp from the roasted garlic, mash with the side of a large knife, and toss with the potatoes. Season with salt and pepper and serve immediately.

Peanut Butter Milkshakes

2 tablespoons smooth peanut butter

4 cups low-fat milk

1 cup crushed ice

1 ripe banana, broken into pieces

Combine all the ingredients in a blender and process until smooth. Serve in medium glasses.

86

One meal that will surely be met with glee by any American child is pizza. These Pizza Burgers are made with ground pork and can be enhanced with many of the same toppings your kids love on their pizza. I would avoid the anchovies and pineapple however! The broccoli and carrot slaw tastes great and satisfies your kids' leafy green and orange vegetable nutrition requirements.

Pizza Burgers with Red Sauce

MENU

o **to eat**

Pizza burgers with Red sauce on Red bread

Italian flag slaw

o **to drink**

Berry smoothie

serves 4

Pizza Burgers

1 pound ground pork

1/2 cup diced pepperoni

1/2 cup cubed mozzarella

3/4 cup crushed Italian-style tomatoes (seasoned with garlic, salt, pepper, and oregano)

1 teaspoon chopped fresh basil

1 clove garlic, minced

Sea salt and freshly ground black pepper to taste

1 tablespoon olive oil

In a large glass bowl, combine the ground pork, pepperoni, cheese, tomatoes, basil, and garlic, and season with salt and pepper. Cover the bowl with plastic wrap and refrigerate for 1 to 4 hours.

Preheat a broiler or charcoal or gas grill to medium-high. Form the pork mixture into 4 patties of equal size. Brush both sides of the patties with the olive oil. Broil or grill the burgers, flipping once, until cooked through and juices run clear, about 4 minutes on each side. Top the burgers with Red Sauce and serve them on the Red Bread.

87

Red Sauce

1 cup crushed Italian-style tomatoes

2 tablespoons tomato paste

Combine the ingredients in a small saucepan and simmer over low heat, stirring frequently, until the sauce thickens. Serve warm atop Pizza Burgers and serve alongside as a condiment.

Red Bread

8 slices Italian bread

2 tablespoons Red Sauce

Brush the bread with a light coating of the Red Sauce. Place under the broiler or on the grill during the last minute of cooking.

Italian Flag Slaw

1 cup plain low-fat yogurt

1/4 cup grated sweet onion

1 teaspoon sugar

1 tablespoon cider vinegar

Sea salt and freshly ground black pepper to taste

2 cups grated carrots

2 cups grated broccoli stems

Combine the yogurt, onion, sugar, vinegar, and salt and pepper in a small bowl and mix until blended. Combine the grated carrots and broccoli in a large bowl, pour the dressing on top, and toss until the vegetables are thoroughly coated. Refrigerate for 30 minutes and serve chilled.

Berry Smoothie

1 cup fresh or frozen raspberries

1 cup fresh or frozen blueberries

1 cup low-fat milk

8 ounces low-fat vanilla yogurt

2 tablespoons honey

Combine all the ingredients in a blender and puree until the berries are no longer chunky, about 2 minutes. Refrigerate until ready to serve.

Veggie Confetti Burgers

Since most kids prefer their veggies well-seasoned and coated, this burger should appeal to all but the most impossible to satisfy. Try to make the burgers as colorful as confetti, and if your kids are exceptionally picky about veggies, try to finely chop the larger ones so they are less likely to be recognized! Be sure to coat the burgers with cooking spray before grilling or broiling to keep them from falling apart. Omit the rolls if you like and serve the burger on top of the pasta.

MENU

o to eat

Veggie confetti burgers on potato rolls

Red pepper aïoli

Pasta with cherry tomatoes and peas

o to drink

Fizzy peach lemonade

serves 4

Veggie Confetti Burgers

1 tablespoon olive oil

1 cup fresh or frozen corn kernels

1/2 cup finely chopped Vidalia or other sweet onion

1/2 cup finely chopped orange or red bell pepper

1 clove garlic, minced

1/2 cup grated carrot

1/2 cup grated zucchini

1/2 cup seasoned breadcrumbs

1 teaspoon ground cumin

Sea salt and freshly ground black pepper to taste

Vegetable oil cooking spray

Heat the olive oil in a large deep skillet over medium-high heat. Add the corn, onion, bell pepper, garlic, carrot, and zucchini and sauté, stirring constantly, for about 5 minutes. Remove from heat and let cool for about 5 minutes. Transfer the vegetable mixture to a large bowl and add the breadcrumbs and cumin, and season with salt and pepper. Mix thoroughly so the ingredients are evenly distributed.

89

Form the vegetable mixture into 4 patties of equal size. Lightly coat each patty on both sides with cooking spray. Reheat the large skillet used to sauté the vegetables. Pan-fry the burgers over medium heat until heated through and lightly browned. Top the burgers with Red Pepper Aïoli and serve them on potato rolls.

Red Pepper Aïoli

3/4 cup store-bought roasted red peppers (liquid discarded)

1 clove garlic

1/4 cup extra-virgin olive oil

1 cup mayonnaise

Sea salt and freshly ground black pepper to taste

Combine the red pepper and garlic in a food processor fitted with a steel blade. Pulse until the peppers are smooth and the garlic is chopped. With the motor running, slowly pour the olive oil through the feed tube. Add the mayonnaise and pulse until blended. Transfer to a serving bowl, season with salt and pepper, and serve. Aïoli may be refrigerated in a sealed container for 1 week. Just stir before using.

Pasta with Cherry Tomatoes and Peas

8 ounces elbow macaroni

1 cup shelled fresh or frozen peas

1 tablespoon red wine vinegar

1/2 cup extra-virgin olive oil

1 clove garlic, minced

Sea salt and freshly ground black pepper to taste

1 cup halved grape tomatoes

2 tablespoons freshly grated Parmigiano-Reggiano (optional)

Cook the macaroni according to package directions until al dente. Drain in a colander and return to the cooking pot.

While the pasta is cooking, cook the peas in boiling water until tender, about 3 minutes. Whisk the vinegar with the olive oil, garlic, and salt and pepper. Add the peas and tomatoes to the macaroni, pour in the dressing, and toss to combine. Top with the grated cheese, if desired, and serve warm.

Fizzy Peach Lemonade

2 cups canned peaches in light syrup

1/4 cup sugar

1 cup cold water

1/2 cup fresh lemon juice

1-liter bottle unflavored seltzer water

Combine the peaches, sugar, and water in a blender and puree until smooth. Pour into a large pitcher, add the lemon juice and seltzer and stir. Fill the pitcher to the top with ice cubes and serve in tall glasses over ice.

In our house, the moment the last mouthful of dinner has been consumed by one of our children, they besiege us with questions about what they can have for dessert. In keeping with the subject of this book, we offer this completely silly dessert burger, which was inspired by my friend Maud during a morning constitutional. It should make any burger-lover smile and any dessert-lover elated!

The Perfect Burger

MENU

○ **to eat**

The perfect burger on All-butter pound cake with Strawberry sauce

○ **to drink**

Classic New York Egg Cream

serves 4

The Perfect Burger

8 slices All-Butter Pound Cake (recipe follows)

1 gallon carton of chocolate marshmallow ice cream, cut into four 4 x 4-inch squares

12 slices peeled ripe kiwi

4 tablespoons Strawberry Sauce (recipe follows)

Keep ice cream in the freezer until ready to use. With a sharp knife, dipped in hot water, cut four squares of ice cream.

To assemble, place 1 slice of pound cake on a plate and top with a square of the ice cream. Top with 4 kiwi slices, 1 tablespoon of the sauce, and another slice of pound cake. Voilà, the burger with pickles and ketchup on a bun!

91

All-Butter Pound Cake

1 cup (2 sticks) unsalted butter

2 cups confectioners' sugar

3 large eggs

1 teaspoon vanilla extract

2 cups sifted cake flour

1/2 teaspoon salt

Preheat the oven to 350°F. Cream the butter with an electric mixer and add the sugar, a cup at a time, beating until the mixture is light and fluffy. Add the eggs, one at a time, beating well after each addition. Add the vanilla extract. In another bowl, combine the flour and salt, then add to the butter mixture, beating until completely blended. Spread evenly in a greased 9 x 5-inch loaf pan. Bake for 50 minutes, or until a fork inserted in the center comes out clean. Cool in the pan on a wire rack for 15 minutes. Remove from the pan by loosening the edges with a knife. Cool completely.

Strawberry Sauce

1 pint strawberries, rinsed and hulled

3 tablespoons sugar

Puree the strawberries in a food processor fitted with a metal blade. Transfer the puree to a bowl and stir in the sugar. Cover and chill for 30 minutes before serving.

Classic New York Egg Cream

1 cup whole-fat milk, chilled

1-liter bottle unflavored seltzer

1/2 cup chocolate syrup

Divide the milk between 4 glasses and pour seltzer into each glass. (Foam will form in the top half of the glass so allow room for it to expand.) Divide the chocolate syrup between the glasses and stir to distribute the chocolate. Serve ice cold with a straw.

93

Index

Pages in italic refer to photographs.

95

Acknowledgments

I am not a professionally trained chef. My kitchen isn't a state of the art commercial catering facility. I shop at whichever grocery store is nearest my other errands, occasionally splurge at the local gourmet market, and use the same pots and pans I got as shower gifts twelve years ago. I don't believe in laboring for hours over complicated food that requires spending more time over the stove than with the guests. I don't believe in inviting people to dinner and feeding them gourmet takeout. I do, however, believe that the way to keep my family together and in touch is to sit down whenever we can at a table with napkins, real plates, silverware, and the time to enjoy food that is delicious and healthy.

I would never have had the courage or temerity to complete this project without the support of the STC crew. A hearty and heartfelt thank you must be extended to my editor, Sandy Gilbert, for her sense of humor, patience with my inexperience and her friendship. In a rare moment of sincerity, I must also thank my dear friend, Meryl Jacobs, who coaxed a proposal out of me, kicking, screaming and laughing all the while, and made me believe I could do it. And thank you at least a million times to Leslie Stoker for giving a freelance writer who loves to cook her 15 minutes.

The visual elements of a cookbook are as essential to its success as the quality of its recipes. I am tremendously grateful to Amy Trombat for her attention to detail and awesome eye for color and design. Tina Rupp and her team of food stylists and assistants turned my recipes into beautiful mouthwatering works of art despite my neurotic hovering and chatter and are all immensely talented and a pleasure to work with.

I attribute my comfort with the written word and the stove to my mother, Marilyn Haft, who managed to make us a real dinner every night and a brown bag lunch every day while holding down a full time teaching job and did it all with such grace and skill all the years of my youth. She taught me three valuable lessons: to trust my own instincts, recipes with two pages of ingredients are rarely worth the effort, and that it's never too early to start planning the next holiday menu.

I never could have tested every recipe in this book without the love, support, and discriminating palates of my husband, Don and two sons, Charlie and Tim. For six months, they ate nothing but burgers for dinner and pulled no punches when asked for an opinion. Charlie asked for seconds even if he didn't like what I had made just to make me feel good and can now make his own burger with ease. Timmy lobbied hard for his favorites and was a willing and patient model for this book. Don made a valiant effort to conceal the Dijon mustard he smuggled to the table during the few less successful experiments and was supportive and encouraging every step of the way. And, I can't forget my faithful hound, Rippy, who minimized cleanup by inhaling whatever fell on the floor (except mushrooms) and could always be counted on to keep me company in the kitchen.

Food stylist: Alison Attenborough
Prop stylist: Stephanie Basralian
Project editor: Sandra Gilbert
Production manager: Kim Tyner

Recipe for Three-Grain Vegetable Burgers, page 68, reprinted from *Totally Dairy Free Cooking* by Louie Lanza and Laura Morton, with permission from HarperCollins Publishers Inc./WILLIAM MORROW.

Published in 2004 by
Stewart, Tabori & Chang
A Company of La Martinière Groupe
115 West 18th Street
New York, NY 10011

Export Sales to all countries except Canada, France, and French-speaking Switzerland:
Thames and Hudson Ltd.
181A High Holborn
London WC1V 7QX
England

Canadian Distribution:
Canada Manda Group
One Atlantic Avenue, Suite 105
Toronto, Ontario M6K 3E7
Canada

Library of Congress Cataloging-in-Publication Data is on file with the Library of Congress.
ISBN 1–58479–352–X

DESIGN BY AMY TROMBAT

The text of this book was composed in Helvetica Neue and Clarendon.

Printed in China

10 9 8 7 6 5 4 3 2 1
First Printing